I MUST HAVE IMAGINED IT

....

I MUST HAVE IMAGINED IT

PAUL JENNINGS

MICHAEL JOSEPH
LONDON

First published in Great Britain by
Michael Joseph Ltd
52 Bedford Square
London WC1B 3EF
1977

1977 by Paul Jennings

ISBN 0 7181 1651 8

Phototypeset by Trident Graphics Ltd, Reigate, Surrey
Printed in Great Britain by Hollen Street Press, Slough
and bound by Hunter and Foulis, Edinburgh

ACKNOWLEDGMENTS

These pieces have appeared (and I list in order of frequency), in *The Telegraph Magazine, Punch, Homes and Gardens, The Times, The Guardian, The Observer, The Illustrated London News, The Sunday Times,* The *Sunday Telegraph, Sunday Express* and *Women.* I am indebted to all for permission to reprint.

Contents

INTRODUCTION

Absolutely my favourite *graffito* (American, of course; the only good English one I have seen with my own eyes was in a Gents at the BBC, saying BEAT INFLATION: STEAL) is one reported in the *New Yorker* some years ago; it said BOYCOTT NON-ACADEMIC POETRY.

According to Richard Findlater's *The Book Writers; Who Are They?* half the writers in this country went to a university. As it happens I belong to the other half, but I'm sure I'm not the only one who wishes there was another study entitled *The Book Readers, and Critics; Who are they?* For that fifty per cent of us who aren't scholars who (I always imagine enviously and doubtless wrongly) speak a special and immediately understood language to a group of initiates, there seem to be two extreme positions. Either the writer puffs out his non-mandarin chest, and with many a fearful jibe at dons and the 'thin blue line of culture', turns out his life-enhancing, red-blooded, rooted-in-the-people work and says to hell with them. Or else, like me, he nourishes a secret fear that if he was really educated and knew everything he wouldn't write at all.

Of course this whole question is meaningless where writers of genius are concerned. Some were educated, some weren't. Dickens didn't go to college, Dostoievsky did—as a student of engineering. When Robert Bridges started his medical training at Barts he had already been to Oxford; medical students had to have either Latin or Greek, and at his first examination he was given a Greek passage and a Latin one, it being assumed that candidates would do the language of their choice; but as there were no

7

specific instructions he did the Latin one into Greek and the Greek one into Latin. Some were teachers, some were on newspapers, some wrestled with the devil for twenty years, one was a tinker, another was a bishop. Obviously there's no general rule for the great.

But for lesser chaps the situation has changed, even since 1942 when Eliot observed, 'you may write English poetry without knowing any Latin; I am not so sure whether without Latin you can wholly understand it.' Even then, you see, Eliot was ready to go a long way towards admitting that the chaps who tell a writer what he has written are as important as the chap who wrote it (the first time I ever heard of this French writer Jouhandeau was in a review that said I was obviously influenced by him. I really *must* read him one of these days and see if I am).

But that was in a presidential address to the Classical Association, in which Eliot was simply making a plea for a traditional and homogeneous culture: he went on to say of Shakespeare that 'never has a man turned so little knowledge to such great account . . . he lived in a world in which the wisdom of the ancients was respected, and their poetry admired and enjoyed.' And perhaps it is true that somehow one can absorb some of that kind of culture by a kind of osmosis. Mr Douglas Woodruff, as a young man, was once in J. L. Garvin's study crammed with books, thousands of books, and asked him if he had read them all. 'No', said Garvin, 'but they're radioactive, dear boy, radioactive.'

But that kind of comfortable classical fug is a long way from the somehow rather cold-eyed, scientifically joyless Eng. Lit. climates of which any writer, educated or not, must surely become aware the moment he stops writing and looks at the ever-increasing output of universities where they have related literature to psychology, history, sociology, politics (and obviously would to science as well if they could) so that it is observed as a kind of machine, of which they know thoroughly all the parts and their functions. Surely a vague unease will take hold of the non-university writer as he looks upon this strange city, a

8

somehow self-contained world, a Chirico or Paul Nash construction full of towers, ladders, patios, receding corridors, where many figures converse among themselves in a melodious and fluting language, perhaps a language of the future (who knows?) which he cannot quite hear.

More and more of these figures will get out of that picture into the real world, for they are undoubtedly real people, who have been to real universities, and know a sight more about the later metaphysical poets or George Eliot's interest in contemporary medical advances than he (the writer) ever will. Many of them will even have been to Creative Writing Seminars and Fiction Workshops (although, God be praised, I've never actually heard of a Humour Workshop). Now and again he will see one of their stories in some rather daunting magazine, usually the characters will have no names but will be just He and She, or The Man and The Woman. As television advances and serious reading shrinks to what it has always been historically, an occupation for that minority for which Ivor Brown uses the word *clerisy,* will these figures (who can now be heard to be speaking English, in that curious accent favoured by most actors, as though someone from Tunbridge Wells with a hot pebble in his mouth were trying to talk Yorkshire) actually take over his world? Will everybody have to write according to rule, in an ever more formalised literary closed shop?

Of course not. A cat may look at a queen. A writer may look at reality, and if he finds while doing so that the new Eng. Lit. world, Cambridge and its ghostly outposts, has been mysteriously radioactive, like Garvin's books, so much the better for him. I hope. I *think* I hope.

I'm sure the boys wouldn't agree with my hypothetical ideal writer figure, which is that of the Surprised Don. It's not possible, of course. Dons are weary heroes back from unimaginable voyages round intellectual space, and whatever they are they are not surprised. The nearest I can think of is Teilhard de Chardin; but much as I admire him, there aren't any jokes in *The Phenomenon of Man*. In real, total surprise there must be an element of delighted

9

laughter as well.

We jokers, who slip through the net of all these classifications, have to retain a certain innocence, to refrain from asking too many reasonable questions, we have to have faith that *all* answers would be incomplete, however knowledgeable the don who gave them. As a crude example, what the hell is Activated Sludge? I once saw these words on a brass plate in Victoria Street, and expanded this question to eight hundred words. Surely you couldn't have two more antithetical words than *activated* and *sludge*? Several angry letters (not, I hasten to add, from the Managing Director of Activated Sludge herself, who wrote a charmer) explained in great details the role of bacteria in sewage disposal.

It's understandable that serious toilers in the field, taking the vast dynamo of sex to pieces or launching their brave rafts on the tossing sea of politics and commitment, should be irritated by this apparent wilful ignorance, this concern with surface contrasts. Our books are scornfully equated with bath salts, they all come out in a great rush in late autumn to catch the Christmas market. Booksellers rig up special tables near the doors of their shops, piled high with our golden laughing moments now frozen into a discouraging mountain of print, like a huge stone meringue. *Come on in, books are FUN*, these tables seem to say to the hordes of dispirited shoppers shuffling past with string bags full of gifts wrapped in special merry paper. Wearily they pick up our books, leaf unsmiling through them, put them down with a small sigh, and move over (often in that same 'bookshop') to buy a soap dog or some place-mats with stage coaches on. Wasn't it Arnold Bennett who used to carry a cheque for £100 which he was ready to give to the first person he saw buying one of his books? And of course he never did. I don't think I've ever *had* £100, but I could manage 50p if I ever saw one of them smile.

It's the same with the reviewing. Not that the reviewers are unkind (hooray), it's the first paragraph of the multiple review that reflects their tormented doubt as to what, if anything, all this has to do with life, or, even more, with

Eng. Lit. This is a standard opening. 'Oh, God, here come the clowns again, tumbling in the sawdust with their fixed and painted grins. There is nothing more dispiriting (depressing, daunting, mournful, unfunny, etc.) than a pile (collection, heap, clutch, etc.) of funny books. Yet still they come, a further giggling (tittering, smirking, cosy, bourgeois, middle-class, middlebrow, whimsical etc.) distillation of the English Sense of Humour. Of course the only real humour is in the unexpected (cruelty, satire, wicked draughtsmanship, *New Yorker*, Jewish idiom etc.). Oh well, let's nerve ourselves and get on with it . . .' I always think it's a good Zen exercise to imagine people who write like that actually telling a joke.

As the review goes on, after they've demolished a few people they say, 'Mr X, however, is the best of a mediocre lot, and although the standard is uneven, sometimes he is quite funny.' We all hope to be this Mr X and so sell 4,047 instead of 4,000. We also feel guiltily that if we want to get a review to ourselves we ought to write a novel, a whole funny novel. But here most of us have a fellow-feeling with the Eng. Lit. reviewers, dons, and other fully-fledged explorers of life; we don't feel funny for long enough.

11

PART ONE

I MUST HAVE IMAGINED IT

....

The other day I got a letter beginning *Dear Panf Smmmmmmmmys* and I wasn't a bit put out. I can quite see how anyone might interpret my signature like that. On another day it could be *Pail Jugus,* or *Pnud Twimniz.*

After all, most people's signatures are a squiggly flourish that doesn't bear much relation to their ordinary writing. We're all used to getting letters apparently from *Ewy Soogl* or *Arf Grlb*.

My case is rather different. Never mind signatures, I can't read my own writing. I can't read my own diaries.

Whenever I read about some notable trial I am struck by the bit about 'diaries now in the possession of the police' being used as evidence. For one thing, I don't believe any criminal in his right mind would use a diary, either to record past crimes *(April 13. Strangled Julia S. Watched Horse of the Year. Very wet & windy),* or to jot down future engagements *(October 21. Break in 6 Windermere Road).*

For another, unless criminals have very much better handwriting than mine, the police wouldn't be able to make head or tail of it. Nor would I, even if I *wanted* to 'help them with their enquiries' (maybe that's what 'helping the police with their enquiries' means). If I were a burglar idiotic enough to put *break in 6 Windermere Road* in my diary, the most I should be able to make of the scrawl two years later would be some such runic phrase as *'breech in to Wirehen Rod'* . . . 'All right, Fingers. For the last time, what did you do with the Wirehen Rod?'

As it is, when I want to help *myself* with my enquiries into anything written down more than two days ago I am instantly led into a surrealist, unrecognisable world.

People in English detective stories are always being asked where they were on Thursday, February 17, and they can always answer. ('Henderson flipped through his diary. "I went straight from Sir Robert's meeting to the Schulbergs' party. You can check with him and the Schulbergs, Inspector." ')

15

I've just looked in my diary to see what I was doing on February 17, and all I can make out is the cryptic entry *11 Dervishes*. I don't know even *one* dervish, the whole thing is a blank in my memory. Yet how could one forget an evening with 11 dervishes, spinning round, faster and faster, in a silken tent in some secret, scented oasis in the Sudan . . . but this is absurd, I've never been to the Sudan. Oh, yes, of course, I see now what it was. *11 Dentist*. How prosaic.

Or look at the entry for July 17. It says *Chombly Donk*.

What on earth could this be? It sounds like something from one of the nonsense poems of Edward Lear, such as the one that goes:

Through the long, long wintry nights
When the angry breakers roar
As they beat on the rocky shore:-
When Storm-clouds brood on the towering heights
Of the Hills of the Chankly Bore . . .

You could easily add:

And the widgeons wail, and the wild geese honk
On that desolate marsh, the Chombly Donk.

Maybe I had a sudden thought that this was the noise that railway carriage wheels make. *Chombly donk, chombly donk, chombly donk.* I don't think so now, but maybe I did on July 17.

Maybe I saw a donkey in a field, with an indescribable expression on its face—indescribable, that is, except by the new-minted adjective *chombly* meaning having its mouth full but looking terribly sad at the same time.

Maybe—but suddenly it comes back to me, I remember now where we went on that sunny day. You won't believe this (but then you haven't seen my handwriting); we went to a *Christening, Dorking*.

Another entry, for April 14, caused me a lot of puzzlement. I couldn't make out whether it was *horse wiseacre, horse riverman* or *horse considers*. All quite interesting, really. When taken as a whole they seem to

16

complement each other. Could it be that on April 14 last year I had some sort of literary inspiration, for a great satirical book where stupid men are contrasted with wise, peaceful, philosophical horses living by some calm river?

Quite a good idea, if only Swift had not got there first, with the Houyhnhnms in *Gulliver's Travels* actually Houyhnhnm is roughly the way the name Hopkinson appears in my writing). In any case I found, by checking against April 14 in *this* year's diary, that what I had written was merely *house insurance*.

Sometimes the reality does turn out to be a bit of a let-down like that. But more often it is the other way round. I get a tantalising glimpse of a strange, science-fiction sort of world peopled by characters like *Grug, Jachius, Ruyns, Weeb* (for this is how the names Gregory, Jackson, Rogers and Webb come out).

Where other diarists have appointments with perfectly ordinary people called Smith, Thompson, Porter, I have been hobnobbing with *Swulch, Thrunkum* and—almost unbelievably—*Puti*. (The crossing of t's looks very much the same as the dotting of i's in my *haudily*—sorry, my handwriting).

Surely Grug is the hero. With Weeb, his comic, cowardly servant, he has many adventures before rescuing the earth-princess Puti from the clutches of the evil Dr Jachius, in league with Swulch and Thrunkum, rulers of a planet inhabited by thinking bananas (called Ruyns) in a plot to rule the universe.

Well, it is more fun than Smith, Thompson and Porter.

If I can't read things like this, written at leisure in broad daylight, it's not surprising that it is even harder to decipher jokes or witty remarks jotted down in the dark at the cinema or theatre, or under cover of the tablecloth at a public dinner.

Once I heard a speaker at a dinner quote something from Robert Benchley. Two years later, when I looked at it, it seemed to be: *Thou buzzest abstract 6 professors and willing toady in the nerrily chagriny the typottle rulber.*

I am sure Benchley would have been the first to point

out that the one thing chagriny could never be in any circumstances is nerrily (however willing the toadys). I had to read a sizeable chunk of his works (a pleasant task) before I found it. 'The biggest obstacle to professional writing today is the necessity of changing the typewriter ribbon.'

Maybe: but don't you think those 6 abstract professors with their typottle rublers run it a close second?

And while we are on great American humorists, what on earth could have been the remark of Thurber's that I have down as: *It had ong our favel, it waa kid of lorry?*

Thurber would no doubt have been as delighted and surprised as I was to find in the dictionary that *favel* means 'the fallow horse proverbial as the type of cunning or duplicity'. But what connection, if any, has this with the baby wailing *waa* (kidnapped?) on the lorry? (And anyway I thought only fields could be fallow, not horses.)

Turns out to have been a characteristic Thurber remark about a play. 'It had only one fault, it was kind of lousy.'

Fortunately, perhaps, my diary is now the only place where I need to use handwriting anyway. Everything else can be typed, provided I remember to type my name under the signature if it is a letter, otherwise I get letters coming to my house for Mr R. Plafftonk or Mr P. Ruggizosh.

The postman never shows any surprise at this. But come to think of it, the clerks in my bank never used to lift an eyebrow, back in the days when the ledger showed the extraordinary payees of my cheques (instead of just the machine-printed cheque numbers, as now). They would hand me statements on which they themselves had typed the information that I had paid £4 to Friend Holy Wills, £22 to Blunt Stern George, and £16 to British Hotch.

These were actually £4 to Freeman Hardy and Willis, for a pair of shoes; £22 to Blue Star Garage for a gearbox job; and £16 to Bristol Hotel.

Did the bank prefer the image of this glamorous customer, friend of legendary nautical characters like Blunt Stern George, to the mundane Smith-Porter-Thompson world of their usual transactions? Or did they, perhaps, rejoice in their sober, bankly hearts, that I was at last showing signs of rejoining that world after an errant youth, with Blunt Stern George, some kind of grave, unsmiling, deep-voiced reformer, coaxing me away from a frivolous career of chucking my money about at the British Hotch (a pretty razzmatazz nightclub), turning my attention to good works, such as Friend Holy Wills, whatever they might be?

Who knows? No life could be too extraordinary for a man called Pnud Twimniz, Or Park Jumper. Or Punt Swimmings.

WINDSPEWT ON HAMPSETAD HETHA

You often hear people say they play the paino by ear. I'm sorry, I'll say that again. You often hear people say they play the *piano* by ear. Well, I play the typewriter by eye. I hace to keep my eye on the keys all the time, unlike proper typists, who have been tuaght at a bussness school, and look at the words as they fly out effortlessly on to the paper.

Touvh-typing, it's called. They can go much faster than I can, and in the rare occasions when they make a mistake they can stop strighat away—*straight* away, and vorrect it, instead of hacing to wangle the confiunded under-varriage back a vouple of lines ecery time, like me.

I should very much like to be a speddy, competent typist like them, but I hace this terrible feelinf it's too late now. I'm sure it is something that has to be learned quite eraly. I mean, of course, it is something that has to be learnt quite EARLY ON IN LIFE . . .

That's another thing about eye-typing; sometimes you go on quite a long way before noticing that the shift-key is still down and you are writing in VAPITAL LETTERS ALL THE TIME LIKE THIS.

It's like ski-ing; if you didn't learn it while you were still young you might as well not try (I can't sko, either).

One obvious drawback is the way that wretched figure 8

19

keeps appearing so often instead of the apostorphe (they are, of course, on the same key). Another is the way the letter m, which is next to the comma, often comes in *place* of the commam like thism producing a kind of hesitant effectm like someone constantly clearing his throat.

But you will already hace notived the worst thing of allm the machine's habit of transopsing adjacent letters, especially the letters c and v. This is probably because they both come under my index fingers on that extoardniraly jumbeled bottom row of keys—zxcvbnm.

This has always seemed to me a very difficuly sequence to rebember. In fact I'm pretty sure that most people who aren8t professional typists couldn't rebember the middle row either—asdfghjkl. On the other hand, anyone could rememer the top line—qwertyuiop.

I have thought of it for years as a real word. It's just possible that Zxcvbnm could be a small market town in Zchekoslovakia; asdfghjkl isn't a word in any language, but qwertyuiop is surely a good omonanomatapaeic word for a corkscrew, the qwert being the squeaky noise as you turn the vork round in the bottel, and the yui-OP being the sound when it comes out.

This brings me to the advatnages of eye-typing. It opens the door to adventures with words that have a subblety of meaning, a freshness unknown to the porsaic ordinary typist. In every pieve I type there are words which could and should enrich the dictionary.

You've only got to look at the first sentence in this article, and there is the word *paino*. Is not this a splendid word for an out-of-tune piano?

Or look at that word that appeared in the second parapgraph—*strighat*. I am sure a strighat is one of those hats with a veil (made of strig, what else?) that bee-keepers have. 'Just gice me my strighat, Emily, I think they're swarbing in the orchard.'

In the old days democracy was defined in the immoral words of Ace Lincoln—'government fo the people, yb the people, fot the people.' But the eye-typist, instinctively in tune with these confused times, is more likely to defind it as: 'goverbmety of the epople, by the opelop, for the pollepop.'

Or look at another word that emerged fresh-minted in an earlier draft of this article, when I said that all these mistakes were driving me *hagwire*. There's a word which ought to exist (well it does now, doesn8t it?). To go haywire means to go straight-forwardly craxy, in an active sort of way, ranting and rabing, throwing your arms about. But to go hagwire is something altogether more glooby and introspective. A person who has gone hagwire has a haggard look, the cornets of his mouth are drawn downwards in his white, strained face. He's probably headed for a sotmach ulcer.

My typewriter refuses to acknowledge the existence of Hampstead Heath. Only *Hampsetad Hetha*. Don't you see this Hampsetad Hetha, a wild region of immense horizons, like the central plain of Hungrya? You can imagine the gyspies breaking in the famous wild horses that roam free on the winspewt Hampsetad Hetha.

I hace often thought it would be a goof idea to start collecting some of these inspirations of the eye-typist. Surely our glotious English language would be even further enriched by the addition of words like *strighat, pollepop, hagwire, windspewt* and such?

There is, however, one insurmounatble difficulty. The moment I tried to type them like that they would come out absolutely vorrect.

WHAT IS LOVE?
(Tick appropriate box)
....

The name of Senator William Proxmire, as any fool etymologist can see, is nearly mud anyway. And now it *is* mud with Dr Ellen Berschied, who heads an American National Science Foundation costing $135,000 of taxpayers' money 'to establish why people fall in love'.

'I believe that 200 million Americans want to leave some things a mystery,' the Senator is reported as saying, 'and right at the top of those things we don't want to know is why a man falls in love with a woman and vice versa.'

Not so, ripostes Dr Berschied. We are not living in the dark ages, we have social scientists now, and this will help them.

God knows they need help, and if they really could find out the common denominator of the love which does not alter when it alteration finds, as Shakespeare put it, this would be a bargain at $135,000. The saving on alimony alone would probably pay for the US Sixth Fleet.

But the senator would surely be on firmer ground if he pointed out that they haven't got a hope in hell, with that kind of money, of even beginning to find a common denominator. It will cost them all of $135,000 just to get the forms worked out.

There will have to be forms, won't there? And they will need to have to be of the neat, check-this-box type, to feed in to the computer. Something like this:

National Science Foundation Project AQ/306/N: Partner Choice Motivation Survey (1975), Heterosexual (for other cases Form S2 should be used).

1. Are you in love? Yes
                      No

2. Are you married? Yes
                      No

3. If the answer to 1 and 2 is Yes, is the person
    to whom you are married the one you are in
    love with? Yes
                No

4. Why did you fall in love? (Check *one* box only)
    Sweet low voice ☐
    Concern about environment, ecology ☐
    Not always going yackety-yack ☐
    Dropped parcels in front of me at
       supermarket ☐
    Good cook ☐
    Eyes like drowned stars ☐
    Great legs ☐

22

Girl next door ☐
Redhead ☐
Her mother not fat, so she won't be ☐
Reminded me of mother ☐
Laughed at my jokes ☐
Beautiful and rich ☐
Beautiful and poor, but what the
    hell, *I'm* rich ☐
She got pregnant ☐
Way she wrinkled nose ☐
Marvellous thesis on Kierkegaard
    What a mind! ☐
Childhood sweetheart ☐
Was drunk at the time ☐

5. Any other *specific* reason. Please write (maximum FIVE words) in the box below avoiding phrases such as 'mysterious chemistry', 'indefinable thoroughbred air'. If genuinely in doubt, put 'don't know'.

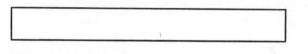

And that's only for men. The ones for women will have to be even longer.

Masterful (sent wine back) ☐
Reminded me of father ☐
Didn't remind me of father ☐
Great biceps ☐
Good job with pension ☐
Wanted mothering (holes in socks) ☐
Pipe-smoker ☐
Was drunk at the time ☐
Reminded me of Gary Cooper ☐
Reminded me of one of the Osmonds ☐
Reminded me of Nureyev ☐
Reminded me of Steve McQueen
Reminded me of Byron ☐
Reminded me of Tony Curtis ☐
    20 years ago, but this *was* 20 years ago

He kept hitting me ☐
Reminded me of Dr Kissinger ☐
Saved me from drowning ☐
Amusing ☐
Serious ☐
Reminded me of some Renaissance prince, with
    his chiselled profile ☐
I saved him from drowning ☐
He had this convertible ☐
Reminded me I was 32, already ☐

Then they will have to make *new* forms incorporating everything that is put in the five-word boxes. Then they will have to start the cross-checking, to see how many couples have loved each other for the same or different reasons. They will have to find out how many people love but are not loved, and vice versa. Watch them, senator, or it will be 135 million dollars before you can say, 'All the world loves a lover, but only the National Science Foundation has examined this phenomenon on a rational basis.'

THE MYTH OF BRIMP

It is high time we had a mythology in Britain. Unlike a religion, which you must believe to be true, a mythology is a marvellous jumbled set of jolly, improbable tales which console you with the thought that whatever people can do, nice or nasty, gods can do more—even while part of you doesn't believe a word of it.

The man-about-Athens didn't really believe that Cronos, son of Uranus and Ge (the earth), castrated his father, and the drops of blood from this operation produced (a) the Giants and (b) Aphrodite, Goddess of Love; that he ate all his male children except Zeus, whom Rhea (his wife) hid till he could grow up, usurp Cronos (serve him right), marry his sister Juno, become king god, and seduce someone practically everyday.

He seduced Leda disguising himself as a Swan, Danäe as a shower of gold, Europa as a bull (Cadmus was sent to get Europa back and then had, for some reason known only to mythologists, to follow a *cow* from Phocis to Boeotia where he killed a dragon and sowed its teeth which turned into armed men who fought till there were only five left and then founded Thebes). Zeus also seduced Alcmene by appearing as her husband (Amphitryon), and you can't get lower than that, even if the result *was* the birth of Hercules.

Then there was all that about King Pandion (later an osprey) who gave his daughter Procne (later a swallow) to Tereus (later a hoopoe) who, however, preferred the other daughter Philomela, who became a nightingale after Tereus had cut out her tongue to shut her up and she and Procne had cut up *his* son, Itys, and served him up in a dish, unfortunately *before* he (Itys) had become a pheasant.

If you said out loud that you didn't believe all this you might find yourself having to drink some hemlock, like Socrates; so you just went rather dreamily along with it, taking it for granted. In this way nightingales, and pheasants, and Thebes, and swallows, and hoopoes, in fact the whole of your everyday life, somehow became more meaningful and poetic.

Now, such mythology as we in Britain have left (mainly King Arthur, mainly Welsh anyway; not to be confused with King Alfred, who is mere history, a very different matter) does not bear much relation to *our* everyday life. So here are a few suggestions for a few legends we could believe/disbelieve in the old happy unity, to replace the boring yah-sucks boo them-and-us feelings that motivate us at present.

Brimp (often called *Bremp* in early texts) was the son of Mars and Britannia, whom he married when he grew up, which he did in one day. He became the ruler of the gods and of the world. *Woad* (his uncle) and *Lud* (his cousin), two giants, were jealous of his power, but after a titanic struggle, in which he was constantly aided by *Marina,*

Goddess of the ocean, he was victorious.

He castrated Woad, all of whose blood was red except one drop, which was blue. The red drops fell on to lands throughout the world, which became that colour on the map for a thousand years. The blue drop fell on the region now called Soho. A thousand films came writhing out of the ground from the spot, and were turned into live shows by the God of Pleasure, *Ty Nan Pornos* (also worshipped by the Welsh and the Greeks).

The *Oracle of Albion,* served by priestesses of the temple near his sacred cave at Wookey, promised that the sun would never set on Brimp's domain, and Lud was confined in another cave a thousand miles beneath the earth at Accrington.

Brimp's eldest daughter *Victoria* sprang fully armed from a cloud of steam at Euston, but in later times her shrine there was pulled down and a magnificent circular temple was erected by the ancient ceremonial Way of Blood (Kensington Gore). It was used by the people for wrestling, music and gymnastic displays as well as religious services and the mysterious Women's Institute rites in early summer.

Victoria was always represented as well-rounded, and the circle was her symbol, the famous 'circle of perfection' in which time came to a stop. The wheel is sacred to her, and she gave mankind the bicycle. Near her temple stands the rocket site from which she ascended to Balmoral, her palace in the sky.

Brimp had many encounters with mortals. Disguised as a merchant he seduced the nymph *India* (discovering too late that she was ten thousand years old). By her he had ten thousand daughters, called memsahibs, who were eventually driven from their country by four heroes called *Laski, Gandi, Gollancz* and *Atli,* and from their tears sprang a great river, the Ganges.

Afterwards Laski became a beaver, Gollancz became an owl, and Atli became a sparrow. Gandi changed sex and became a woman (*Mrs Gandi*) after a battle with the hero *Churchill,* who afterwards became an eagle. Mrs Gandi

26

ruled India for a thousand years because of her famous riddle. Many princes and revolutionary heroes came to her country and fell in love with her, or it. She would then ask them 'what is democracy?' If they did not know the answer they were imprisoned in a cave for a thousand years, and if they did know it they were executed.

Disguised as a mayflower Brimp also seduced the nymph *America,* his own daughter by Marina. She bore him two children, the hero *Boston* and his sister *Philadelphia.* Boston, while still an infant, planned to steal the secret of *cuppa,* the drink which made Brimp immortal; but *Tivi,* the Messenger of the Gods, warned Brimp, who was thus able to trick Boston into stealing an inferior substitute which could not produce the trance-like stillness, the god-like ecstasy, of real cuppa, which enables true worshippers of Brimp to remain motionless, far from the cares of the world, for long periods every day. In his rage Boston emptied the substitute, known as *tea,* into the ocean, where Marina turned it into salt.

Meanwhile Brimp, disguised as an architect, *Dublin-Georgian,* attempted to seduce the nymph *Hibernia,* but was foiled through the jealousy of Marina, who sent a perpetual rain cloud in which Hibernia could hide. It also turned her green.

When he grew up Boston was raped by Hibernia, by whom he had ten thousand small sons (minutemen) who grew up into dragons' teeth. After many heroic tasks Boston was taken up into heaven on a cloud of respectability. The bean and the cod are sacred to him. Philadelphia became the Goddess of Symphonic Music.

Brimp also became enamoured of the nymph *Industria* when he saw her bathing in the river Tyne. She was the daughter of *Vapor,* God of Railways, who lived in a palace of iron. A brother of Britannia, he was angry at the liaison, and he broke off pieces of his palace to throw at the pair wherever they met, usually in the northern part of Britain. However, Brimp's magic shield, *Ignorance,* protected him, and the pieces of iron fell harmlessly to earth, where they became factories.

27

They also enraged Lud in his underground northern kingdom. He burrowed under the earth from his Accrington lair to London where, taking advantage of Brimp's absence in India, he surfaced and proceeded to build, with the help of his dwarfs, a circular citadel *(Ludgate Circus)* and to lay claim to the Sacred City.

Brimp's vengeance was swift and terrible. He buried the entire city under monstrous stone blocks (called *towers*). Lud retreated underground, but not before snatching *Prosperina,* youngest daughter of Brimp and Britannia. She was the bringer of warmth to mankind, the Goddess of Money, Central Heating and Holidays. Now her beautiful temple, the *Stock Exchange,* was filled with wailing priests in their ceremonial *top hats,* imploring her to return.

Lud, however, was implacably resolved not to release her unless he was allowed to destroy the factories which, through Brimp's affair with Industria, had covered his northern, gloomy land.

Moved by the prayers from the Stock Exchange and the annual sacrifice of a hundred economists, Brimp eventually came to an agreement whereby Prosperina could return to the land once every fifty years and Lud was allowed to destroy the old factories, and any new ones that appeared, during the other forty-nine.

The hero *Tuc,* offspring of Lud and Prosperina, performed many heroic deeds in *Tolpuddle, Clydeside, Dagenham, Coventry, Blackpool* and other places, slaying monsters called *bosses.* He too was taken up to heaven, on a cloud of votes, and became a god. Before long it became clear that, like many previous gods, he wished to castrate Brimp himself. But Brimp, warned of this by Tivi, craftily allowed Tuc to drive the chariot of the sun on its daily journey round the earth, warning him on no account to stray from the path laid down by the fates *(Fates)* from time immemorial. . . .

THE GAME OF THE NAME

Many peoples, after a down period, seem to have

recovered themselves after changing their currency—France and Germany, for example. It wasn't de Gaulle who gave the French their new confidence as much as that New Franc, worth a hundred of the old ones.

That doesn't seem to have worked with us, when we had the Dismalisation of the Currency. In fact one new p, technically worth 2.4 old pennies, seems to buy about what you could get with one old halfpenny. And the only use for the new ½p that I've ever found is for screwing the little slotted thing on my electric razor over from 220 volts to 100 on the rare occasions when I've managed to get to a 110 volt country (once, to be exact).

Anyway, what kind of a name is that for a coin—just a letter of the alphabet? Whitehall being what it is, it's probably only a matter of time before they simplify matters still farther by calling the pound an a, the 50p a b, the 10p a c, and the ½p a d. We shall move even farther away from the solid, historically resonant sound of names like *crown, sovereign, florin* (originally from Florence), let alone the exotic golden *guinea*.

Matters have probably gone too far, actually, for giving our mere currency more inspiring names (the franc, after all, does embody the name of the country); at this juncture it would be no good having the *brit,* or even the *eng,* even if Scotland does bring back the bawbee and the plack. We need more far-reaching measures. It is time for one of those grand, sweeping gestures that the British surprise the world with from time to time (like having a Revolution more than a century before the French, or inventing the industrial system, or cricket, or producing Shakespeare). It is time *we,* not the mere currency, had new names.

You've only got to look at a book like the *Penguin Dictionary of Surnames* to see that long centuries have dulled the sharp sense of identity, of a person's skill, place of origin, adventure, occupation, physical peculiarity, or whatever, that gave him the name which he passed on to increasingly remote descendants. If you gave Mrs Thatcher a *leggat* or told her to get on with her *yealming* an uncharacteristically blank look would come into those

29

blue eyes, although these are terms well known to any thatcher. *Wilson* merely means, of course, Son of Will (except in a few rare cases, it says, connected with Weevil/Beetles Farm in Leicestershire. H'm).

Scargill means, believe it or not, 'valley/ravine with mergansers'. A merganser, according to *The Oxford English Dictionary,* is 'any bird of the genus *mergus,* fish-eating ducks of great diving powers, with long narrow serrated bill hooked at the tip, inhabiting the northern parts of the Old World'. You can see where the miners' leader, still diving away in the northern parts of the Old World, got it all from, although it's the nation that now has to pay the long bill, not serrated at all. But it seems a little . . . well, fanciful; and as for Mr Heath, the brightly-lit concert halls and warm crowded bookshops where his time is now passed seem a world removed from the bare, windswept uplands from which his ancestors were named as they huddled behind gorse bushes from the driving rain, like King Lear and his fool. *The Penguin English Dictionary* does contain Macmillan ('son of the shaveling/baldhead/ tonsured (servant)/tonsured (religious) Scots Gaelic, 50th commonest surname in Scotland in 1958') and Attlee ('at the wood/clearing'); it doesn't give Callaghan at all.

In any case, so many people are named, for instance, after occupations that—to take the most obvious example—you don't exactly give anyone a sense of identity by calling him Smith, or, for that matter Lefevre (French), Schmidt (German), Ferrari (Italian), Herrero (Spanish), Kuznetsov (Russian), Kowalski (Polish), Kovacs (Hungarian), Haddad (Syrian) or Magoon (Irish).

We did make one attempt to start again in the 17th century, but that was strictly in the context of the Puritans, with such names as Faint-not Hewett, Tear-the-devil's-breeches Snodgrass, Through-much-tribulation-we-enter-the Kindom-of-Heaven Crabb, Fly-the Harlot Hackenschmidt, Kill-Sin Pimple, and Stop-Thy-Snivelling-The-Lord-is-Come Hawkins (I have actually made up three of these, and the others are real; you are invited to guess which, and looking at page 160 of *The Personalities of Language* by Gary Jennings, published by Gollancz in 1965, is cheating).

Many original names in earliest tribal days simply came from something that happened to their owners; He-Who-Sat-On-A-Scorpion, She-Who-Lay-With-The-Minstrel, He-Whom-The-Tree-Fell-On, that kind of thing. Perhaps the time has now come when we could combine all these elements in a re-naming process that would allow us to escape from our tired, centuries-old view of ourselves and start again.

We do, after all, live in a time of ferment. We emerged victorious from the war against Beast-With-Moustache, under our great leader Oak-Heart-Cigar-Smoker, although it was only with the help, eventually exceeding our own effort through sheer numbers, of Wheelchair-Man and Ogre-With-Biggest-Moustache—both of whom, for different (or perhaps ultimately the same) reasons, wished to relieve us of our Empire which in any case we had begun to have doubts about after being morally upstaged by I-Bet-My-Loincloth-Is-Holier-Than-Thine whose traditions of freedom have been so admirably upheld in that country today by his daughter-in-law.

So the time is apt for an exciting new look at ourselves, for sweeping away old social divisions under an all-embracing social plan worked out by Receiver-of-The-Divine-Breath-of-The-Webbs, giving security to all from the cradle to the grave. A new election put the Up-Hands-Down-Brains Party in power, led by Bald-Warrior-of-Few-Words (originally At-The-Wood-Clearing). His economic policies ('export or die') were directed by Thou-Shalt-Find Salvation-In-Austerity.

Foreign relations were handled, at first with great success, by Bluff-Aitch-Dropper-On-Purpose; but, as the opposition (Horse-Owning) Party pointed out, there were fewer and fewer fields remaining open to us for independent foreign policies; ironically this was forcibly brought home to the nation at large when they were in power again, under Persian-Scholar-Who-Named-A-Hat, whose every move against Ersatz-Pharaoh-the-First at Suez was

31

blocked by America's Pebble-Glass-Stone-Face.

There followed a somewhat hectic, inward-looking period of false prosperity, presided over by the new leader of the Horse-Owning Party, Old-Walrus-Warrior (formerly Son-Of-The-Shaveling/Baldhead-Tonsured-Servant). His interim replacement, High-Class-Skull, was thought to be a pheasant-shooter and port-drinker too remote from the people, and this led to the Premiership of Sailor-Who-Took-Smiling-Lessons.

In the second half of the Sixties and the first half of the Seventies a fascinating duel developed between him and Pipeman-with-All-Answers, who had earlier beaten Blue-Suit-Quasi-Miner and Red-Haired-Money-Teacher to the leadership of the Up-Hands-Down-Brains Party (another possible rival, the Biogwapher, having been given a post in Europe, which we had managed to join after the death of its leader, Dieu-C'est-Moi-Le-Plus-Grand-Homme-Du-Monde).

Meanwhile the real great issues—the Separation of the Kingdom and the Closing of All the Shops—which are to determine our future, in which it is hoped that no one will have to work at all except those who get oil from the Scottish Ocean, have been coming to a head; and two fresh leaders of the parties have emerged at this crucial moment, Ice-Queen-with-Two-Degrees having replaced Sailor-Who-Took-Smiling-Lessons, and Invisible-Stoker being our new Prime Minister.

It is an exicting time in art and sport, too. An enormous complex, Theatres-of-Unknown-Celebrities, run by Small-Beard-One, has opened on the South Bank, across the river from another famous national theatre run by Small-Beard-Two. Small-Beard-Three, a famous footballer once with Manchester United, delights his followers whatever division he plays in. After a dip in our national football fortunes from the time when we won the World Cup under Grim-Football-Leader-From-The-South, the new manager, Grim-Football-Leader-From-The-North, has shown our age-old courage in shrugging off a defeat by Italy and pointing out that the Cup is miles off yet, probably over four years.

All we need is a continuation of the social contract, complete re-equipment of our factories, an end to the brain drain, the long-expected collapse through overwork of Japan and Germany, and with our new-minted identities we shall come to the top again, prospering like Little-William-Ho before you can say Jack, Son of Robin. It might fox the computers, but who cares about that? We never needed computers when we ran the world in the days of Old-Queen-In-Lace-Cap-Who-Was-Not-Amused.

HISTORY FROM STAMPS

The story of the 10-snerd commemorative of Sloj is fairly well known. In 1848, the European 'Year of Revolution' the seething discontent of the oppressed watchmakers of the tiny kingdom came to a head. Under the autocratic rule of Jakab III watchmaking was a royal monopoly. All watches were made in the royal watch factory at Prznz, and to their already high cost price was added the hated watch tax of 100 krnks, which found its way straight to the royal coffers.

In earlier days Sloj was famous for its watches and clocks. In fact it was the great Slojian horologist Jvn Smrz (1701–1769), commemorated in a bicentenary issue set last year, who invented the neck-watch, precursor of the wrist-watch as we know it today. It was really a small clock, attached to the end of a bracket on a hoop, called the zmoly, in such a way as to be clearly visible to the wearer. It was operated by a weight which slid down a guide-cord attached to the belt to stop it swinging about.

Long after the neck-watch was superseded by the wrist-watch the zmoly, which rapidly assumed a highly decorative character, and was often finely chased like a Celtic torc when worn by aristocratic watch connoisseurs, became a traditional part of Slojian national costume, as did the belt, intricately studded, called simply the Smrz, much as we named the Sam Browne after its inventor.

There are two beautiful examples of the Smrz in the Victoria and Albert Museum, and of course the zmoly is shown on the 5-snerd sepia of the bicentenary set.

But to return to the 19th century. The royal watch monopoly was repressive in several ways. Thousands of watchmakers were thrown out of employment because of the suspicious Jakab's policy of importing docile but largely unskilled labour from Borenia to replace the skilled but strongly independent natives. Moreover the high prices of the watches, never less than 150 krnks, put them beyond the reach of the ordinary man, who was lucky to earn 500 snerd, i.e. half a krnk, in a month. Thus only the rich employers and landowners ever knew what the time was; a peasant starting his day's drudgery at 6 a.m. would be upbraided for lateness and told that it was already 7.30, and similarly it was always possible to squeeze an extra hour or so of unpaid labour at the end of the day.

On top of this was the continuing affront to the national pride of the Sloj watchmakers, forced to look on in idleness as the inefficient royal industry laid an international reputation in ruins, paving the way for the Swiss to take over the supremacy which they still hold. Many managerial posts went to court favourites quite ignorant of watchmaking, and the thriving export trade dwindled when customers found they had got a watch with no minute hand, or two minute hands and no hour hand, or even a perfectly normal-looking watch in which, however, the hands went round anti-clockwise. The modern Sloj word for 'anti-clockwise' . . . *jakabsrnzl*—recalls this.

The story of the abortive attack on the Prznz factory by a crowd of watchmakers and peasants led by Tazym Zbonsz on June 13th 1848 has provided Sloj with many classic issues. The 2-snerd airmail of 1952 shows the insurgents, led by Zbonsz with a company of clockmakers armed with heavy pendulums, with the Prznz factory, grim and fortress-like, in the background. Warned by informers, Jakab had ordered the dreaded Opmi dragoons to lay an ambush. Pendulums and other crude weapons were no match for rifles, although the red 50-minmy first issued in

1948 shows, in heroic-realist style, a rifle-clutching Opmi reeling backwards before a fiercely bearded clockmaker swinging his pendulum.

Zbonsz was seriously wounded, but in the confusion he was carried into the factory by sympathisers. The first 1-krnk stamp ever issued, the famous 1902 green, depicts the famous night escape in woman's clothes when Jakab's police, becoming suspicious from certain captured letters, searched the factory some months later. Zbonsz had spent the whole period recovering from his wound in the escapement department (the word's happy punning significance occurs in Slojian also; 'to escape' is *zatarjn,* and 'an escapement' is *zatarjnszl*). Here he was tended by Mvri Kdeli, the beautiful Borenian girl who, after many hardships and adventures, eventually became his wife.

Her part in the escape was discovered and she was imprisoned. Zbonsz made his way to America, where he worked tirelessly for the Free Sloj cause. He was able to do this the more easily because of the fortune he earned by turning his inventive watchmaker's mind to the development of a steam typewriter (1853), depicted on the Zbonsz centenary 5-snerd (1922), an ingenious machine well ahead of its time, since there were no ordinary typewriters till the 1870's, although somewhat bulky (it was some five feet long).

In 1856, well supplied with funds, he secretly re-entered Sloj and set about organising a more effective opposition to Jakab, whose regime was going from bad to worse. But here again he was betrayed by an informer and arrested. He was sentenced to death, and the sentence would doubtless have been carried out despite the strong representations of the U.S., Britain and many European powers, had not fate intervened with Jakab's own sudden death and his succession by the mild, reformist Prlpil IV.

That enlightened monarch's first move was to release Zbonsz, his second to declare an open watch industry, and his third to permit the first elections in Slojian history.

In 1873 he became the country's first prime minister and it is here that the curious story of the 10-snerd commemorative begins. There was of course an entire set, ranging from 1-minmy to 500-snerd, to celebrate this important constitutional change. In view of the weakness of liberal-populist governments following that of Zbonsz, leading to the bloody take-over by the military under General Kruk twenty years later, there have been historians who declared it weak, not democratic, of Prlpil to allow memories of armed revolt, however justified, to be revived on the country's postage. Be that as it may, all the 1873 issue bore an overprinted legend '13 June'—the date, of course, of the revolt against Jakab. Philately was then of course in its infancy even in London and Paris, and was virtually unknown in Sloj.

It was in fact an English philatelist, the Revd C. E. Dromgoole, who noticed that the overprint on the 10-snerd was '31 June'. Wisely (in the event) refraining from pointing it out publicly he wrote to Zbonsz pointing out the error (for this he was subsequently made Grand Knight of the Candlestick with Clasp, Hasp and Thing For Getting Stones Out of Horses' Hooves, the highest order open to a foreigner). On investigation Zbonsz found that the manager of the printing works responsible for the stamps, a man called Jrs Zrgly, was a member of an extreme right-wing organisation dedicated to overthrowing Zbonsz and restoring state watch monopoly. He was planning to alter the overprint on all the stamps to the date '31 June', which of course does not exist. It was an act well calculated to appeal to the Sloj sense of humour, which is somewhat different from ours, and to discredit Zbonsz with ridicule.

True to liberal tradition, Zbonsz did not punish him but merely had his ears cut off, dismissed him from his post and burnt his house to the ground, with a clemency he may well have regretted twenty years later when Zrgly was Kruk's right-hand man. About 40,000 of the '31's' were printed and only half of these are accounted for officially. Present market value is around £15 each, so it is interesting to speculate how it would be affected if a vast hoard of the rema ning 20,000 were discovered—and there has always been a persistent rumour that such a hoard was made by none other than General Kruk, a keen philatelist when he was not massacring watchmakers in a confused period of the troubled history of Sloj. But that is another story.

NASCIENCE

London, January 1, 2030

There is much for us to feel grateful for today, on the fiftieth anniversary of the World Republic, and it will do no harm to the spirit of that Republic if we in County Britain indulge in a little self-congratulation for once. Indeed, at the Guildhall banquet last night Mr Swaraji, our Indian Prime Minister, paid eloquent tribute to the British breakthrough in Non-applied Science, or Nascience, as it came to be known, which in the sixties and seventies of the last century led to the world's first Ministry of Limitation and the subsequent restraint of science and the sublimation of war into an intellectual game of the highest subtlety.

Earlier in the day Mr Swaraji had driven in state to visit the international shipping dressed overall in the Pool of London. No doubt the scenes en route—the cheering crowds who had poured in on horseback, by diligence or electricar—were duplicated by similar greetings to leaders in a hundred countries on this great day of celebration, greetings to the Greek Prime Minister of Germany, the American President of Russia, the Cuban President of America, the Russian President of China, and even the French Prime Minister of France.

Yet, among the great four-masted clippers, the elegant paddle steamers, and the fussy little hovercraft, all gaily decked with flags, one had a residual and not unworthy feeling of pride that it was the case of a British ship, the Hermes (an 'aircraft carrier') which led ultimately to the abandonment, in the nick of time, of a science that was leading the world straight to annihilation.

The Hermes was built in 1959 at a cost of £18 millions.

On March 9,1964, *The Times* carried a report that she was to be withdrawn for a two-year refit to enable her to take a 1,600 mph aircraft called the Phantom II, and also said: 'the refit will not approach in scope the Eagle's four-year modernisation programme . . . only three carriers will be operating throughout the 1970's and the Hermes will be one. The others will be the rebuilt Eagle and a £60 million ship authorised but not yet ordered . . . when the Hermes is completed the dockyard will begin a £5 million adaptation of HMS Blake, the £14,900,000 cruiser which was "mothballed" after one commission.'

In the event the Hermes never put to sea again. Halfway through the refit the Americans scrapped Phantom II for Phantom III, which could do 3,000 mph (although only for two minutes), and the refit estimate was revised to £110 millions. Meanwhile the preliminary designs of the other authorised carrier (the £60 million one) rose, in anticipation of the 4,000 mph Phantom IV, to £136 millions.

It was this ship, never actually built or even named, that was the turning point. The success of HMS Blake had led advanced Admiralty thinking to the daring experiment of mothballing *before* commission, and since the cost of mothballing had now risen to £59 millions, it was but a short step to not building at all. Why not give brilliant scientists and designers free rein by allowing them to work unhampered by economic and physical limitations?

Since the object of all peacetime military planning is not so much actual war (always greeted with pained surprise) as making the other side feel they are being left behind, it was not at first revealed that the new carrier, as redesigned in the 1978 estimates (of £470 millions) to carry Chimera III ICBM's, was now purely theoretical. But it caused Russia to scrap her plan for 25,000 submarines: and when in 1984 she announced that work had already started on three £870 million carriers, each with equipment for 100 planes capable of circumnavigating the world, *and* building a space mirror that could focus the sun's rays on any part of the sea containing capitalist ships and boil it, rendering them immobile and vulnerable to large anti-tank guns, an international conference was called to see if anything could be done about the whole babyish business.

It was not attended by America, whose vast material resources enabled her to go on actually building ships for nearly ten more years till she, too, was on the verge of bankruptcy.

Science knows no frontiers, and, in the friendly international atmosphere of many of the world's top scientists at the conference, Britain boldly placed her cards on the table. The gamble succeeded. The Russians cheerfully admitted that even preliminary work on their space mirror carriers would set their economy back ten years. It was at this conference that Nascience was really born, as the scientists argued endlessly about whose ship could beat whose if actually built, and out of these arguments grew the quadrennial International War Games, an intellectual equivalent of the Olympic Games.

The American triumphs at last year's event are a signal tribute to her intellectual vitality in making up the ten years' leeway caused by the shackling of her finest brains to the confining realm of the practical.

At that historic conference the absorbed Nascientists were rudely disturbed by crowds outside Lancaster House shouting, 'Down with Applied Science!' By 1984 the automation necessary for practical technological superiority was a real threat to human personality, denying ordinary men the chance of satisfying work as well as threatening them with atomic annihilation. Our Ministry of Limitation was set up in the same year, to restrict the application of science to a few innocent necessities such as the operating theatre, the hovercraft, the electricar. And as scientists in other countries, (freed from technocratic power urges), became attracted to the pure delights of Nascience, their governments followed our example. And the rest we know.

DRY LEGAL LIFT

It was the kind of really heavy rain in London that makes

39

one feel a cross between Mr Micawber and a tramp; an outsider, an irresponsible summer butterfly suddenly up against the real facts of life. Oh, it was all right until today having no hat or umbrella, wearing shoes which let water in. Windy grey riverside blocks, buses in sunlight, up stairs into first-floor offices, taxis to dodge the odd shower, pub doors at noon, autumn trees in squares, even glimpses of parks—one mixed on equal terms with the vast life of London, one had real business in it, just like anyone else.

But now! Compared to those odd showers, this business-like and all-permeating rain was like the Blitzkrieg after the Phoney War. People with whom I had lightly joked were now withdrawn into dry, solid offices, their typists made them cups of tea while they gazed out at dead leaves swirling in the gutters, before returning to serious files. Taximen, knowing which side their bread was buttered, drove past the despairing shouts of the odd beggar like myself huddled under some streaming doorway, they swished importantly to known or secret buildings in the City, where known, real London men with umbrellas and good shoes would hail them and enter dry-shod.

It was too wet for bus queues; but whenever a bus appeared (with some useless number like 76, going God knows where—some secret domestic haven, some neat suburb with tea kettles already singing), efficient men and women with umbrellas, their lives organised so that the 76 *was* their bus, would materialise from under sheltering walls and step briefly through the tempest as the bus, *their* bus, drew up.

In any case, I was far from any bus stop, even a 76. I was sheltering in a court of gloomy arches, having just come from an obscure meeting in some obscure legal buildings at the wrong end of Lincoln's Inn. It rained so loud I couldn't even hear the typewriters clicking. From time to time some legal gent would come out, open his umbrella and walk to an elegant car parked under the sodden plane trees.

Actually I only had to go about 600 yards, to the Kingsway Hall, where Dr Klemperer, Elizabeth Söderström and three other distinguished soloists, Leslie Pearson (organ), the New Philharmonic Orchestra, 232 members of the New Philharmonic Chorus (I am No. 233) and EMI recording engineers, all miraculously bone-dry, would soon be looking at their watches and saying, 'Tchk, tchk! We can't possibly start the great fugue from the *Credo* of the *Missa Solemnis* without *him*.' But they were 600 busless, taxiless, peculiarly exposed yards, mostly across the great open square with no protecting buildings.

Well, come, decisions! The only possibility seemed to be to walk on the outside edges of my shoes and wear a great paper hat which I would make from a newspaper; and if I encountered one of those lawyers with umbrellas I would give him his money's worth, perhaps mumbling incomprehensible runes, or gabbling and shouting curses.

The hat would be, of course, not of one sheet, but the whole thickness (it was 12 sheets) of the newspaper. Surely that would last 600 yards. It is years since I have made a paper hat, and I had an obscure recollection that you must start with a square. I laid the paper down, folded one corner diagonally across and tore off the remainder. I thus had a 12-fold, 2 ft square and 12 sheets 3 ft by 1. Perhaps they would make some sort of lining.

I never got anywhere near a hat, let alone a lining. I got all sorts of interesting forms, but nothing that would actually stay on the head. Once, quite by accident, I got a boat. Whenever I got anything that looked remotely like the paper hat of childhood it was sealed at the bottom—a one-dimensional hat, as it were. I thought of tearing a slit, but I knew a proper hat is made by just folding; tearing might produce a paper chandelier, or a dragon mask, or 12 elegant little boxes.

Suddenly a gust of wind blew through the gloomy little place like an open-air crypt, smelling of stone and rain. It caught the unguarded 3 x 1 pieces and whirled them about. A man who might have been a judge came down a turret staircase as I was retrieving the last of them from the bottom step. *PM Plans Ginger Groups,* it said. I saw them as groups of about seven, dotted about, twitching and

41

nodding, in an apathetic landscape; dancing frenetically with their trouser legs rolled up, making sudden darting, purposeful marches holding up the traffic. . . .

For a moment, I thought of asking the man if I could borrow a hat, or maybe a wig. But he spoke first. He said, 'I know how to make a paper hat. But perhaps I can give you a lift?'

And he did. I just hope he *is* a judge.

OH, THEY DO LIKE TO EAT BESIDE LA MER

The British tourist abroad should always remember that Continentals are rational and we are empirical. This doesn't apply only to technical philosophy—the watertight, clockwork systems of men like Descartes or Sartre as opposed to our own Locke, forever worrying about the act of perception, or all those men at Oxford today, wondering what words are and whether you can say anything at all, let alone with Continental style. It applies to everything—architecture, food and, particularly, behaviour on the beach.

We approach the sea, that great vague nothing that confronts land as the unknown confronts the mind, with haphazard, instinctive behaviour. When it is warm enough we show the sea a great undifferentiated swarming mass of families and individuals, each doing nothing or something, dozing in deckchairs or playing free-form cricket, as whims of the moment dictate. All is unplanned, improvised; the empirical response.

But people go to Continental beaches with a rational, prearranged plan. They are brought up like this from earliest youth. The reason there seem to be more orphans than parents on foreign shores is that as children they all go in huge school and orphanage parties, wearing blue shorts and floppy white hats. They march about with nuns or students, singing rhythmical songs. They swim, to many whistle-pheeps, in enclosures made by connected cork floats in the sea. In everything there is procedure, everything is more so than it is here. The people on our beaches are unclassifiable, one and one. But in the rest of Europe they belong to one of three basic groups: Children, Eaters and Exercisers.

The segregation of the children, as noted above, means that the Eaters can really organise themselves, in huge family parties which are often centred round one or more grandmothers. There are two or three fortyish brothers (or two families may join forces), fattish, balding, and their wives, who are usually not fat but have very short upper legs so that they *look* fat in bikinis, but they do not mind, they are all jolly and brown and laughing. There are one or two younger couples, possibly grown-up children and their betrotheds, gazing into each other's eyes, withdrawn among the laughter and light music from the very good radio. There are enough adults in the group to account for a score or so of children but all they have here is one toddler or baby.

And they are certainly equipped for eating. They have a whole dining room out there on the sand; umbrellas, awnings, tables and chairs, cutlery, glasses, very often an icebox (you don't catch *them* eating sandy gobbets of bread and processed cheese). You never actually see them setting all this up, it always seems to be just there, whatever time you arrive.

It is obviously not worthwhile for a British family to lug all this furniture abroad, even if they possess it. There remains, therefore, the third group, the Exercisers. Clearly, the casual visitor is unlikely to fit into anything like the many formal games of water polo, played by men in tight-fitting caps with many cries of *Pfui!* and *Wheesh!* (or perhaps more accurately *Ouiche!*), or the complete soccer matches of young men which move up and down the beach, constantly threatening the elaborate tables of the Eaters but never somehow upsetting them; or even the *pétanque* (a kind of bowls where the most unbouncing ball in the world, made apparently of lead and iron, is nevertheless not bowled but thrown) with which the Eaters gently aid their digestion when the sun loses its fierce

43

afternoon heat, while the grandmothers get the coffee and apéritifs ready.

There are, however, many simple, basic exercises which will enable the British visitor, once he has attained the right colour, not to stand out too noticeably. For individuals, there are *Solitary Gymnastics*. Sooner or later, the most paunchy man or the coolest and remotest beauty will get up from sun-bathing and do anything from headstands and cartwheels to a few serious-faced press-ups. For pairs of girls there is the *Five-Mile Walk*. This is undertaken without conversation or communication of any kind, in the stretch of some six hundred yards at the water's edge, up and down at quite a fast clip, so that the same two girls will pass any point some fifteen times. For two men and a girl, less often two men and two girls, there is *Flinging the Quoit,* a heavy rubber ring which the recipient should always be able to anticipate because great play is made of feinting at the third player. This is sometimes played with a ball instead of a rubber ring; but the ball is used more often in *Cat in the Middle*. This game is of course played here, but whereas we eventually allow the person in the middle to catch the ball, on Continental beaches the game retains a fixed structure, with the girl in the middle and the men at either end throwing it impossibly high. Unlike the soccer players, this girl is allowed to kick sand into Eaters, etc., in her efforts to gain it.

There is also the *Dash into the Sea,* an exercise naturally popular in warmer water than ours. This consists of a run down the beach at absolutely top speed, straight into the water, a tremendous falling forward where it is two feet deep, and six ferocious strokes of the crawl, followed by meditation, standing stock still.

There is also of course actual *Swimming*. But that is the same anywhere.

IT'S EVERYBODY'S PIDGIN

Here is the beginning of an essay by a 13-year old boy

which a teacher friend showed me. 'Actually quite a bright boy, and not dyslexic,' he said.

'We hab a nis hodla and wet torcey me dedan mume me sicte lurt to sim in the se the we som big waws . . .'

You have to have been teaching for some time to know that this means: 'We had a nice holiday and went to Torquay (with) my Dad and Mum. My sister learnt to swim in the sea. There were some big waves . . .'

Here is something a bit better, since you expect something a bit better from anyone hoping to do a Music O-level:

'A snarter is a composition written for one or more instruments. When it is written for three instruments it is called a shmpe. The great snarter writer was Betehoven. He wrote 62 pags of snarters. The phathque op is 13 has three movements. The first is in snarter form. It has expisition, development and decapitulation.'

This is a clearer communication, although it assumes a readership able to make the intuitive jump from *Phathque* to *Pathétique* and from *shmpe* to *symphony* (one must admit this with some regret; *shmpe* would be a very good word for some of those modern compositions, all gongs and cymbals, when you long for them to get to the decapitulation).

For an increasing number of people now, this kind of thing is near enough:

'In anser to you avertisment I wish to aply for the tempry posision in your controll labotery. I have two A levels Physics and Chemistry . . .'

Not, presumably, in English, although even if this had been among the applicant's attainments there is no certainty that it would have been all that much better. After the brilliant false dawn of universal compulsory literacy there *was* a brief period when everybody knew how to spell *symphony* and *laboratory,* or they did not get very far. But the unpalatable fact is that in order to exercise control over anything as rich, diverse, and full of infinite potential as the English language you need rules. And rules need learning. And the only way to make most people learn them is to bang them very hard on the knuckles with a cylindrical black ruler every time they get anything wrong, up to the age of about 14.

Well, we can't do that any more; and meanwhile the proportion of yacking to writing has increased a thousand-fold, a huge flood slubbering all over the precise moulds of the written language and squashing them out of shape. The quacking flow comes out of the walls, from lighted screens, handbags, car fascias, rowing-boats, woods, fields, caves, deck-chairs, trains, lifts, bathrooms, bedrooms, even cemeteries.

Even without a transistor you can almost feel this torrent of unstructured words trembling about you in the air. Sooner or later it will burst through and start babbling in an incomprehensible jumble on wire fences, iron gates and railings, even keys, wristwatches, ear-rings; any bit of metal it can find. Then the next big invention will have to be some kind of portable neutralising box that can silence a few yards around its owner.

Many of the people who do this yacking have grown up in the post-cylindrical-ruler-on-knuckle days. They are dimly aware that somewhere there are, or were, rules. But the few pedants upset about it are not very for*mid*able to ordinary people; thankfully it is now a super*flu*ous con*tro*versy, it would be a diabolical liberty to try to make everyone talk proper . . .

Surely the time has come to stop trying to bridge the ever-widening gap between written and spoken English. Why don't we go the same way as they did in Old China, and let popular spoken English go on its own way, independently of the carefully preserved written language?

The more I look at pidgin English, the more it seems to me to offer a vivid, ready-to-hand language which, with a very few additions, would answer all the needs of popular communication. What could be more expressive than 'apple belong stink' for 'onion', or 'gubmint-catchum-fella' for 'policeman'? Or 'grass belong face' for 'whiskers'?

It is said that 'halt or I fire!' used to be: 'you-fella you stand fast. You no can go walkabout. Suppose you fella walk-about me killim you long musket.' Rather long-winded for an emergency; but there are enormous longueurs in, for instance, cricket commentaries, which would be charmingly filled by this kind of thing:

Edrich stand longtime he do nutting, sametime ball-fella Lillee tell im field go here go there, he make im one-two-three belong slip. Time we watch im, me ask friend belong me in talk-box, what time him other fella bat belong left hand make ten-by-ten in one-two hour Thursday. You look im in book belong bimeby (book of old records) *Jim. Yes, him book say J. R. Snogsworth belong left-hand, make ten-by-ten leventh day Shower Time* (April) *one-two-six year by Jubilee belong Queen Victoria* (i.e. 1893). *Now Lillee him start run.*

And think how much more interesting even humdrum things like the weather forecasts would sound:

Tomorrow you-fella by sunset land (the West), *catch im plenty rain belong sea. You fella in deep land sometime catch sun, sometime catch water, you fix im hat belong head or wind catch im you lose it. You-fella other side belong sunrise you all-time lucky bastard, catchim sun all day, catchim rain in night.*

As a matter of fact, when you come to think of it, a great deal of *written* English (if you can describe government publications as written) would sound better, and could be read out on the media, in this form. Take that booklet on inflation that came through everyone's letterbox the other day:

ATTACK ON INFLATION. A POLICY FOR SURVIVAL. A guide to the Government's programme. *Flight im big debbil, big money get little ting. Make do for keep on living. You follow im walk-about belong Gubmint.*

I don't know, though. Even now I can see the end of it. The mandarins who had held on to the written language would feel, as the generations went by and the gap became ever wider, that their duty was increasingly plain; to bring the glories of our literature to the masses. So they would set to work on translations, beginning of course with the classic passages:

To be, or not to be, that is the question:
Whether 'tis nobler in the mind to suffer
The slings and arrows of outrageous fortune,
Or to take arms against a sea of troubles,
And by opposing end them?

Bin or no bin, you ask im? You tink more good, carry in by you head stone belong string him bad fella throw it, carry im arrows belong bad debbil luck? You tink fight by dem troubles belong sea, make um all-time stop?

On the other hand, of course, they might bring back the cylindrical black rulers.

BUT IT *IS* A CONSTABLE, CONSTABLE

Several times in news stories about the fake Samuel Palmers I noticed the words 'the Art Fraud Squad'. Everyone has heard of the ordinary Fraud Squad, probing yet another pillar of the City, or Socialist contract-wangling, or Soho, or whatever. But *art*?

I should like to think that we've never heard of them before because most of the time they are left well alone, in a suite high up at the Charing Cross end of New Scotland Yard, where they enjoy not only a north light but also extensive views of the river from the wide studio windows. In recent years a small laboratory has been added but it is not much used; for X-rays, carbon tests, pigment analysis and the rest of it, they prefer to rely on the resources of the main Forensic Laboratory.

Grizzled, bearded Chief Inspector Max Prothero, in sombre mood on his return from the weekly meeting of departmental heads, glances up at the motto over the entrance to the familiar, comfortable, shabby old Art Nouveau room before entering. It is from Aristotle: *we must represent men either as better than in real life, or as worse, or as they are. It is the same in painting.*

The quotation, like everything else in the room, dates from the time of the famous Commissioner Horatio Trenton, creator of the AF Squad, the only policeman in the New English Art Club, to which he graduated via evening classes at the Slade; friend of Sickert—and unmasker of famous Edwardian forgers like Dodger Miles ('Durer' mezzotints), Willie Hunt (the 'Birmingham Botticelli'), and the notorious couple, Fay Louise Jenks and Oliver Crompton, whose Vermeer factory at Carshalton deceived half the world's museums.

Prothero, surveying the huge room, with four constables and a sergeant working at their easels in the last of the winter afternoon light, reflects sadly that his long fight to keep it this way, with real policemen properly trained in the techniques of copying, is coming to an end. On just such a day thirty years ago Trenton had said to him, 'Imitate the imitators, that's the way to do it! Read yer Aristotle, me boy!'

The sergeant, Dewi Llewellyn, recently promoted for his brilliant uncovering of a Swansea gang turning out 'recently discovered' works by David Jones and Ceri Richards, sees at once that something is amiss. 'You been having another battle, with the Philistines, Inspector bach, I can see.'

'Light the gas, Dewi, there's a good fellow,' says Prothero wearily, 'and let's have a little Pernod. I need it. You're quite right. The devil of it is, they're so *illogical,* one can't reason with them. You know how I've fought for years to keep this Squad a genuine part of the Yard, with men who have proved themselves as ordinary policemen, passing our own internal examinations here in art forgery. I always resisted intake from the universities, straight into officer rank, after the Trenchard reforms.'

'Have they been on about Constable Dalrymple again?'

'Yes. You know he was one we *did* take from outside, just to satisfy them. He did Fine Arts at the University of East Anglia, wherever that is.'

'But he's terribly keen on the job, and quite content to start as a constable. I'm sure everyone in this room would agree he proved his worth in the Case of the Missing Mondrians.' There is a general murmur of assent.

'Quite so. I don't pretend to understand abstracts;

rhythm schmythm, how can you tell one from another? But these millionaires go for them, and it was his discovery that the little yellow square was in the wrong place that saved the art buyer of Neiman Marcus in Dallas from losing nearly a million dollars, put Pincher Snodgrass behind bars, and got us a bouquet from Interpol.'

'I suppose they were on about him having to wear uniform, as usual.'

'Yes. Just because he *is* only a constable, and because our establishment only allows one sergeant—and that's *you,* Dewi, no offence!—Internal are insisting that he wears uniform at all times.'

'But that's not fair! There are plain-clothes men, detective constables, not of officer rank, in other branches.'

'Just what I said. They're only doing this to try and force amalgamation with the general Fraud Squad, all those frightful auditors and people. They're jealous of our identity, our separateness. They keep saying we just sit about here. It's useless trying to explain to them the need for constant research and keeping up with modern forgery technique, as well as going out after forgers.'

'But we do, Inspector bach, we *do* go out! Cosmo, Cyril here—all of us do it. Shadowing anyone who spends a suspicious amount of time copying masterpieces in the musuems. Mingling with the customers in low artists' cafés near the V and A and the Tate—aye, and the Lever Art Gallery in Birkenhead, the Barber Fine Arts in Birmingham; even Glasgow.'

'Do you think I didn't tell them all that? But no, they said. Uniform at all times. I asked them, what use would Archie Dalrymple be in uniform with a foot of that gorgeous blonde hair, like the aureole of some flaming Pre-Raphaelite god; but all I got was coarse laughter. Tell him to get it cut, they said. Where is he, by the way?'

'Out on a job. Got a tip-off at the National.'

'Was he in uniform?'

'Of course.'

'They'll get away then. As usual. Even if he had cut his

hair. I asked them, what the hell would be the use of a uniformed policeman with close-cropped fair hair in a low artists' café? That's your problem, they said. I tell you, Dewi, sometimes I feel like . . .'

The bell beside the candlestick telephone shrills urgently. Wearily Prothero picks up the earpiece. Then he stiffens as the hasty whispered message comes through. It is from Constable Dalrymple.

'Archie One here. Sir, we were right about that woman copying the Botticelli *Annunciation*. She finished it today, and I followed her to a mews flat behind Harley Street. The door was opened by a smooth Levantine with dark glasses. I'm pretty sure it was the Beirut dealer who sold the so-called Sketch for the *Primavera* to Sheikh Oman.'

'Where are you now?'

'In the telephone kiosk opposite the BBC. Nearest one I could find. I ran like hell, because I think they're going to scarper very quickly with it. I had my cloak on over this damned uniform, but it must have opened as I ran, they saw I was a policeman. Their look-out man followed me. He's in a car now, waiting in Riding-House Street. I think I saw him aiming a Beretta till he saw me looking. Can we get the nearest squad car on to him . . . he *is* on double yellow lines, and I look *mad* twitching about in this box so he can't be sure of his aim.'

'We'll handle this ourselves, Archie. Stay where you are. Stare him out, with a hand under your cloak, as you were taught; he'll think *you've* got a gun.'

Prothero puts the phone back on the hook. 'Come on, men,' he grates. 'We'll show them whether the Art Fraud Squad are real policeman or not. Here are your truncheons. Dewi, get the horse into the hansom straight away.' Past experience has shown that this vehicle, once owned by Horatio Trenton himself, cuts a way through the traffic, as admiring motorists pull to one side, with a speed impossible to mere police cars. In no time, filled with burly and determined men of the Art Fraud Squad, it is clattering along Whitehall to the rescue of their comrade and the apprehension of yet another forgery gang . . .

At least, I hope it is. If not, they might just as well be *ordinary* policemen, mightn't they?

THE GLEAMING-EYED ACCOUNTANTS

I cannot for the life of me form a clear view of the sort of people involved in this advertisement, which I keep seeing in all the posh papers, with slightly varied wording; this is how it was in the Financial Times:

> The Gaslight, 4 Duke of York Street SW1. Day 01–734 1071, after 8 pm 01–930 1648. Tonight—do your entertaining at the Gaslight. Your clients will approve and your accountants will be impressed. Exciting Cabaret. Lots of feminine company. No membership for out of town and overseas visitors.

It conjures up a quite different picture of accountants from the normal one. If I were a business man (and I am sure that being the managing director of Jennings Patent Suspension Bridges, or Jennings & Willett Small Wire Things, or even just Paul Jennings, Italian Riding-boot Importers, with lovely trips to autumn leather fairs in places like Milan or Perugia, would be a damn sight easier than writing, 'where', as Ezra Pound observed, 'one needs one's brains all the time') I shouldn't want to impress my accountant; I should want him to impress *me*.

'Get me Gribble and Peacock, Miss Hathersage,' I should bark, flipping a switch on the intercom. No, 'get me Gribble and Peacock, *Daisy*.' Temps would have come and gone, but plump, calm, fifty-ish, blondish Daisy Hathersage alone would have stayed the course, admiring, in her gruff way, the famous tantrums of 'The Guv'nor'.

'Now see here, Gribble, what's all this tosh I've had from the Inland Revenue about F.O.A. procurement vouchers not qualifying for import drawback at face value? I've got an S.407 here for nearly £4,000. Why the hell didn't you claim under Section IV(a)? . . .'

'I'm dreadfully sorry, Mr Jennings. I've been away,

with my stomach, and I'm afraid young Redvers hasn't dealt with F.O.A. back float guarantees before . . .'

'Well, I'll send the papers over, and you'd better sort it out by the 15th or I'll be looking for a new accountant . . .'

Evidently the boot is on the other foot with the people who go to the Gaslight. Henry Phipps, London manager of the old-established Walsall engineering firm of Johnson & Groocock, runs his hands anxiously through his thinning grey hair. On the wall there are pasted several advertisements cut from engineering magazines of the fifties for machines which 'can be adjusted to perform Swaging, Wiring, Ogee Beading, Bottom Closing, Paning Down, Joggling or Necking, Crimping and Beading, or Jennying and Flanging'. But Phipps is staring morosely at an untidy pile of correspondence.

'I simply can't understand how we can have an S.407 for nearly £4,000, Miss Hathersage,' he says wearily. 'Do you suppose Gribble has overlooked it?'

'I'm sure it's only a hitch, Mr Phipps,' she says soothingly. 'We have sold so many of those machines this year, we can't surely be in debt. And that nice young Mr Padgett, from Amalgamated Flange and Bracket, telephoned while you were out to say they're very happy about the tender for the Friction Bolster Snubbers. He's in town for a few days, he said he'd pop round about four to discuss a few small details. Let me make you a nice cup of tea.'

She walks across the shiny old brown linoleum to the gas ring behind the bentwood hatstand. As the kettle boils there is a knock on the door and Frank Padgett comes in. He is a rising young executive with styled and shaped hair and very grand shirt and tie.

'Henry, I've been wondering how you manage such competitive tenders; I can tell you in confidence that you were nearly £3,000 under Grummetts, your nearest rivals. But I can see one reason is you keep the overheads down, with an office like this.'

'Well, I believe in essentials, Mr Pa . . . er, Frank,' says Mr Phipps. 'But I have got some rather good sherry in the

53

safe. If you'd care . . .'

'No thanks, I could just do with a cup of that nice-looking tea. Been tanking up all afternoon at the Peeperama. Smashing show, it's called *Airs without a G String*.' He winks at Miss Hathersage's back.

His practised eye takes in the S.407 at a glance. When Phipps explains his troubles he says, 'Gribble and Peacock? But they're Dickensville. You want a good sharp lot, like Grish, Devine, Fronks and Meatyard. They actually had the Inland Revenue paying *us* for two years. There isn't a dodge they're not up to—nominees, holding groups, Cayman Islands, the lot. Why don't you take Tom Devine out, soften him up a bit?'

'I suppose I could try. Miss Hathersage, would you get me the National Liberal Club, please, and see if you can book a table for . . .'

'No, no, you won't impress him in an old morgue like that. Tell you what, I'm going to the Gaslight tonight with Bill Grish—we were classmates in Business Studies at Loughborough. Why don't we make a party?'

Bill Grish turns out to be a young man much like Padgett. Tom Devine is a kind of imitation Guards officer, with gap teeth, a toothbrush moustache, world-weary eyes, a smart light grey hound's-tooth suit, and an effortless command of the languages and tax laws of several countries. Wentworth Fronks is a rotund man in a blue suit, eyes lecherously gleaming behind pebble glasses. Oliver Meatyard, the senior partner, has a white goatee.

Mr Phipps, looking as worldly as he can, pushes through a surly crowd of Australians in bush hats, Arabs in burnouses, Scotsmen in kilts and Yorkshiremen in bowler hats, trying to look like Londoners and get in.

'You'll enjoy the Atmosphere here, Mr Meatyard. It's, ah, rather exclusive. No membership for out-of-town and overseas visitors, you see. Now, what would you like?'

'Lots of feminine company, heh heh heh. Ah, my dear, can you do the veleta?'

'Champagne all round,' cries Mr Phipps recklessly, 'and make it snappy, before the exciting cabaret starts.' He is

54

wondering when would be the best time to bring up the subject of S.407's . . .

So am I, still.

THE QUARREL PSYCHOLOGICAL

Ever since I read the story about a psychiatrist, Mr Dougal Mackay, telling the British Psychological Society conference at Leeds how he taught couples to quarrel *from scripts* (and afterwards make it up in bed) I have been worried about what happens if they get the wrong scripts:

he arguments might seem very contrived and mechanical at first with the scripts, but then we find them producing arguments themselves for the first time.

The couples, usually in their early thirties, come largely from the upper middle class or the working class.

With one it is the stiff upper lip of the British tradition to withhold emotion. They come from the stockbroker type belt and rarely talk to each other except at cocktail parties.

With the working class it is probably related to the parents who shouted too much at each other, or perhaps they got beaten up or they were smothered by mother. . . .

Scene One
The lounge at Coathangers, home of Rex and Belinda Cox-Fysshe-Hart. They have just returned from a cocktail party. Belinda throws her mink stole on the floor and sits down stiffly to read the Tatler, while Rex stares moodily out of the French windows.

Belinda: For God's sake say *something*. You said enough to Venetia Sopwith-Benson at the de Howards.

Rex: I see Penang Rubber picked up a couple of points today.

Belinda: Oh, for God's sake, show some aggression, be a *man!*

55

Rex *(wearily, picking up script):*   Oh, very well. *(Reads)* 'ere, wot's the use of me workin' me bleedin' head orf all day if I can't have a drink wiv the lads? Wot about you going down the bingo every night then? Where's me bleedin' supper then?

Belinda: Is that what you were doing with Venetia, your funny imitations?

Rex: Dr Mackay said we weren't to ad lib till after next session. Stick to the script.

Belinda *(she has the right one. Reads):*   Does it never occur to you that a woman might feel warmed by some amusing flattery?

Rex *(Reads):*   Ow, shut yore cake-ole.

Belinda: What a *bizarre* expression! What *do* you mean?

Rex: I don't know, any more than you do. It's evidently some kind of expression people use when they're quarrelling.

Belinda: You can't have picked it up from Venetia, then.

Rex: Less of your lip, or I'll bash yer. *(Laying aside script)* I say, dash it, Belinda, that's a bit orf. You know what Lucy de Howard is like. She collared me as soon as we got there and said, '*Do* talk to poor Venetia, Rodney's just left her.' And anyway, you seemed to be makin' out all right with Miles Choate-Harbinger. Never *seen* you so animated.

Belinda: You know dashed well people of our sort rarely talk to each other except at cocktail parties. Why didn't you talk to *me*, then? *(She picks up Rex's script by mistake and begins to read stiffly from it):* I'll tell yer strite, if you fink I'm goin' ter sit 'ere all night makin' apple pie and darnin' yore bleedn socks, like wot your mother did an' 'all you've got another fink comin'! So jus' you . . .

Rex *(seizing script from her):*   No wonder you dropped out of RADA in the first term, dear. Ha, just as I thought, this is the wrong script. Look here, it

56

says on the top, Joe and Nell Gluggett.

Belinda: Trust you to pick up the wrong one. Joe Gluggett. *(Dreamily)* I wonder if they're that couple I've noticed in the waiting room. She's a fluffy little thing, he's very swarthy, always has a check shirt open down to his waist, a very *physical* look about him. . . .*(Fade to . . .*

Scene Two
The living-room at 3 Tolpuddle Close, Stansgate New Town. Joe and Nell Gluggett are much as Belinda described them. Years of work as a bodge-grouter on building sites (he is 32) have given him a magnificent physique, which years of beer-drinking are now causing to sag slightly. She has the pert look of the kind of housewife always depicted on television commercials as smiling at the milkman.

Joe: Ar, come on, gi's a kiss then.
Nell *(reading)*:   Desh it, look heah, does it nevah occur to you that a woman maight feel warmed bai some amusing flattery?
Joe: Wot the 'ell are you talkin' abart?
Nell: Wot's the use of goin' dahn the clinic if we don't do wot 'e told us? We got to 'ave a proper quarrel.
Joe: Me mum was allus quarrellin' wiv me dad, an' you know wot 'e done? 'E took 'is belt to 'er, is that wot you want?
Nell: No, you got to read the script.
Joe *(who has the right one)*:   I *was* readin' it. You don't think I *want* ter talk like that after a 'ard day at the groutin', do yer?
Nell: An' a 'ard evenin' at the beer, you mean, while I been sittin' all alone on this bleedin' new estate. *(Resumes reading)* Ai would much rawther hear harsh, unkaind words from you then none at all. Ai em more than a sex-object, ai em a *person,* and the soonah you realise thet the bettah.

57

Joe: Cor, you never talked like that when we was down the Buildin's. Wassermarrerwiyer, it don't say that on my script. Gi's a look *(Seizers her script)* 'Ere, you've got the wrong bleedin' one, you stupid little . . . *(He is just about to strike her when there is a loud mellifluous two-tone bong from the door-chimes).*

Nell *(looking out through the lace curtains)*: 'Ere, it's that feller was in the waitin' room last time we was down the clinic, got that toffee-nosed thin-faced woman with 'im. *(She crosses to mirror over fireplace and stands on the orange and purple hearth-rug primping her hair.)* Cor, I look a sight. *(To Joe)* Go on then, let 'im in. *(Exit Joe, sounds of male conversation in hall.) Re-enter Joe, with Rex.*

Rex: Ah er oh er, herm herm, ah, Mrs Gluggett, ah, er, bit embarrassin' bargin' in like this, ah herm herm, been explainin' to your husband, me name's Cox-Fysshe-Hart—

Joe *(sotto voce)*: That ain't a name, it's a bleedin' telephone directory.

Nell *(in a curious strangled voice)*: Charmed, Ai'm sure. Would you care for a cup of coffee?

Rex: Oh, aherm, yers, very kind actually. *(She makes no move to go and get it. There is an awkward silence, broken by Rex)* Deuced embarrassin' in fact, but I think we got each other's scripts.

Nell *(aside, to Joe)*: Go on, you make the coffee, you know where the bottle is. I'll talk to him *(Exit Joe, scowling).*

Rex: Hope you don't mind my mentionin' this, but you don't look the sort of person to be in the sort of trouble, aherm, my wife and I, er . . . well, I mean, this charmin' room, it all looks very cosy . . .

Nell: Oh, you'd be surpraised. Mai husband thinks Ai'm just a sex-object *(reading)*. We hev to

58

realaise the existence of the gulf before we can
start to build the bridge.

Rex: I say, you put that frightfully well. I should
frightfully enjoy building a bridge bewteen us.

Nell *(nervously, but not displeased)*:   Wot the 'ell's 'e
doin' in there, 'e's a long time with that coffee.
*(Exit to kitchen, where there is no sign of Joe,
because of . . .)*

Scene Three
*The lounge at Coathangers. Joe standing awkwardly in
doorway.*

Belinda: *Do* come in. Haven't I seen you in Dr Mackay's waiting room?

Joe: Yus. Yore husband came down, 'e said we'd
got the wrong script. I come up to bring yores,
but I've left the ruddy thing be'ind.

Belinda: Just as I thought. Beautiful pectoral muscles.
Never mind, darling, we shan't need a silly old
script . . .

Now they'll all *really* have something to quarrel about.

LIB LAB LOBBY
....

Sir,—The election manifestos of all three parties reveal a
no doubt studied aloofness on a crucial issue—whether
Britain will slavishly follow the European practice of
driving on the right now that we are in the Common
Market.

Apart from the obvious correctness of our method (most
people are right-handed, therefore a right-handed car is
logical) such a course would show cynical ingratitude to a
body of men who have served the road travelling public
well for a number of years. As their representative may I
ask all motorists, coach and bus travellers to make sure
where their candidates stand on this vital question. I am,
Sir, your obedient servant,

59

Samuel Chubley

Secretary, Association of Garages on the Left-hand Side of Roads out of Large Cities.

Arterial House,
North Circular Road, London.

Sir, The economic and political promises made at this time by those with the ambition to govern us are either incomprehensible and dull or comprehensible and unfulfillable. All the true democrat can do in this complex situation is to test his candidates on a simple matter of the rights of minorities in this great land of ours. I refer to all men who, through no fault of their own, have thick necks.

Every time I buy a shirt with the correct neck fitting the sleeves are six inches too long, and for my part I will vote for any candidate who will support legislation compelling manufacturers to remedy this, and I call not only on others with thick necks but on all who love fair play to do the same.—Yours faithfully,

Norman Twilgarth

Parchment Lane, Uttoxeter.

Sir,—Once again the politicians try to tempt us with their indistinguishable pies in the sky. Let us at least see this time that we get a fair deal for men with long arms, who are so unjustly penalised by appearing all neck when they buy a shirt of the correct arm length. A simple piece of legislation would ensure that the manufacturers turned out a reasonable quota of long-armed shirts.

Although shirt manufacturers are mainly Conservatives this Association has had no real encouragement from the Labour Party either, and I therefore suggest that both sides should remember that many floating voters have long arms.—I am, etc.,

T. Ranson Farson

(Secretary, Association of Men with Long Arms)

Grimbley Chambers,
Cranbottom Lane,
Leeds 6.

Sir,—During the last Government's period of office the image of Her Majesty the Queen on our stamps has been replaced by what appears to be that of Miss Shirley Temple in her late twenties. I trust that patriotic voters will draw their own conclusions.—Yours,

(Rev) T. Charles Hatfeather

The Vicarage,
Small Chuckling,
Nr. Quiddy, Som.

Sir,—How much longer must the alphabetically under-privileged of the country, those whose names begin with letters from N to Z, wait for justice? At every stage in life, from school lists of swimming parties, through army pay parades, to the position of their poems if they appear in an anthology, they are discriminated against. For nearly thirty years now the Alphabetical Order Reform Society has pressed for a measure, as simple to operate as daylight saving, establishing Z to A as the statutory order on odd dates.

If all parties continue to ignore these claims it is only fair to warn that we shall be forced to initiate mass deed poll action with its attendant chaos as thousands scramble for such names as Aaronson, Aab and Aal.—Yours very truly,

Y. Zyzki

(Chairman, Alphabetical Order Reform Society)

Hardbody Chambers,
Great Scott Street, London.

Sir,—Every time an ice-cream van approaches this village
with its dulcimers blaring, more molehills appear on our
once beautiful lawn. It is the same everywhere in this
district, and many of us believe the noise in some way
excites the animals. I wrote to our MP to see what could
be done about this nuisance, but no action was forthcom-
ing. Moreover, my husband now finds it impossible to buy
muffins anywhere. We have voted Conservative for many
years, but now we are beginning to wonder.—Yours
faithfully,

      Sylvia Cront

Ramblings,
Quantum Posset,
Dorset.

Sir,—The iniquitous VAT has all but obliterated the
ancient craft of bun-fuddling. Moreover the few remaining
bun-fuddlers, nearly all self-employed, are denied
purchase-tax relief on haulmers, kedge-rings, cranting
blocks, and other essential equipment which quickly wears
out.

  British bun-fuddling was once world-famous, and as any
Dickens reader will know, was enjoyed by all classes. Let
voters to whom a well fuddled bun is one of life's
consolations remember this.—Yours,

      Amos Thundy

The Old Bakery, Sidings Lane, Blearby, Lincs.

Sir,—The party that abolishes the damnable tight trousers
of today, by whatever means, gets my vote. Millions of
man-hours must be wasted by men having to take their

shoes off to change into old gardening trousers (do no politicians ever garden?). At the moment these are old enough to be wide enough to be taken off again while still wearing shoes; but well within the life of the next Government today's tight trousers may themselves become the old gardening trousers, so that twice as many man-hours will be wasted. *Verb. sap.*—I have the honour to be, sir, Your obedient servant,

Neville Gringeley-Sale

Etwas, Salop.

Sir,—How many more of these letters are you going to print?—Yours, etc.,

Paul Jennings

Hill House,
Rectory Hill,
East Bergholt, Suffolk.

THE MODEL WORLD

After a prolonged study of fashion magazines I have come to the conclusion that modelling is a very undercrowded profession. As far as I can see there are only nine models in the whole of Britain. I have come to think of them as Diana Proudface, Barbara Bones, Sarah Sullen, Laura Wispy, the teenage Sulkpot Twins (Butch and Titch), the Hon Penelope Thynne-Mouth—and two men, Simon Likely and Max Saturnine.

There are millions of people in London alone, all different not only from each other but from the people I personally know (at least 500 if you include the chorus in which I sing). An infinite, inexhaustible variety of faces is available to the photographers. But is this variety reflected in the fashion magazines? No. All you see, over and over, are these nine basic figures.

63

If it is a posh indoor show, whether in London or Paris, Diana Proudface will be the star of it, beside the flowers at the bottom of the swirling staircase, wearing the terrific ball gown or the classic suit for lunch at Maxim's.

She is always alone. Barbara Bones and Sarah Sullen often have to share the picture. If the collection has something pretty daring or see-through it is usually Sarah Sullen, with her smooth, brushed-back hair, pencilled eyebrows, deep-set eyes and general don't-you-*dare* expression, who has to wear it, looking about as sexy as a pillar-box.

The Hon Penelope Thynne-Mouth is the one with the spaniel in winter. It always seems to be February, and she wears a camel-hair, sheepskin or suede coat. In the background, out of focus, there is the terrace of some great country house, or the elms of the home wood against the skyline, or a racecourse, or some moors. And always, in the foreground, the spaniel or the labrador.

Laura Wispy often has a dog too, but it is something much more romantic and elegant: a saluki, a borzoi, an Irish wolfhound. She has a fondness for birch groves and often wanders into them with this dog, wearing something trailing, with polka dots. Sometimes she's right out there on the moors, or on some rocks by the sea, got up to kill for a dinner party and obviously lost, or in a trance, or both. The other guests are probably all ready to sit down, miles away. 'Where's Laura?' someone asks (probably Simon Likely, a slightly vacuous clean-shaven youth with plastered-down hair). 'Gorn orf with that dorg,' says Penelope Thynne-Mouth, 'no use waitin' for *her*.'

Actually Laura isn't the only one who has to wear clothes unsuited to the background. They all have to do their stint of beachwear outside Buckingham Palace, evening dress at an abandoned tin mine, tennis togs in the rush hour at Charing Cross. But she is the only one who doesn't look thoroughly disenchanted. She never actually smiles. None of them do (in this they are the exact opposite of the people in TV commericals, who never *stop* smiling). They mostly look either angry or bored.

Well, you can understand the Sulkpot Twins getting restive after endless sessions, wearing striped woollen stockings, apache sweaters, long skirts and berets, under old railway arches or outside derelict houses in Wapping. But it's no different when they're off to the Caribbean to model bikinis. They look just the same, pouting under the palms. They lie stiffly on the coral sand, or in the gentle warm surf, or (perhaps wearing shirtwaists and those funny long shorts) they lie back in complicated leisure chairs on a verandah, or sip an evening gin in a hammock, looking as though they'd missed the last bus from Runcorn on a foggy night in January.

Often they seem to be scowling at something or someone just to the right or left of the camera, and I am beginning to wonder whether this is Max Saturnine, and they are all somehow in his power. It is true that Max, good-looking in a sneery kind of way—dark, a chiselled mouth, cleft chin—does now and again appear as a model himself, usually wearing a dark blue blazer and either pouring out a drink in an offhand, sophisticated kind of way, or (unlike the girls) staring straight *at* the camera, looking sinister. But somehow he looks as if he is in control of the whole thing.

Is it because of this that wherever they go there is an air of mute rebellion about them? Obviously, for instance, there is some rule about no boyfriends. Very often the girls do manage to smuggle out messages about the next assignment, and that is why you see Barbara Bones and Sarah Sullen in that pose like a lookout on the fore-deck of a sailing-ship; one leg in front of the other, knees bent, the body straining forward, one hand shading the eyes as the horizon is anxiously scanned.

But not for land. Whether it is outside some dazzling white façade of a baroque church in Brazil, or a Greek monastery, or an Indian temple, or by some railings in Kensington, they are looking for boyfriends, *any* friends who will come and take them out of this, and back into the normal, million-faced world.

But no help comes. Whatever power it is that Max

Saturnine wields, it is pretty inpressive, because he seems to wield it over the local population as well, wherever they go. You would think that if you put a pretty girl in a swim-suit or play-clothes or an off-the-shoulder number in heliotrope organdie among Clydeside riveters, or lusty Spanish fishermen, or Indian peasants with bullock-ploughs, a few eyes would turn, a few wolf-whistles be heard. If she were set in the streets of Naples you'd be wise to expect more than that.

But no. Either the locals totally ignore these exotic creatures in their extraordinary attitudes, or in the bottom right-hand corner of the picture there *is* one man looking at them rather apathetically.

Photographers being the fusspots they are, it is possible they have been there for so long waiting for the sun to come out, and all the other things that have to come right for the photographers, that they are now part of the landscape. But I don't think so. There is something cowed, tamed, about the onlookers, as though they had been either bought off or threatened off. Could it be that this Max runs a huge photography Mafia, complete with heavy mob and terror? Is that why no outsiders, with ordinary faces, dare muscle in?

Perhaps he and the Hon Penelope run it between them. It is noticeable, as we have seen, that she only actually models in February (the close season, really); and she never seems to be on these foreign trips either. That, incidentally, is why the girls get away with at least one bit of rebellion which a woman would notice but which escapes Max Saturnine—make-up. The older girls wear none at all, so as to appear haggard and drawn; but the Sulkpot Twins absolutely daub it on—great gashed mouths, inexpertly rouged or dead-white cheeks, coal-black eye-shadow, false lashes, orange fright-wigs—like a five-year-old who has got at Mummy's dressing-table.

Penelope, in fact, runs the office side of things and takes the money to the bank during the months that aren't February. In between trips they all live in that country house, with a diet strictly supervised (like everything else)

66

by her. Barbara Bones and Sarah Sullen won't last for ever, and one of the things that the Sulkpot Twins know is coming to them is that one day, when suitable replacements for the teenage market have been press-ganged, *they* will be put on the thin-gruel-and-lemon-juice diet which is all Barbara and Sarah get.

And it's no good poor, feeble, inbred Simon Likely trying to run away with Laura Wispy. Those moors behind Penelope's house are treacherous, and Max and Penelope, who have other dogs beside those spaniels, would be after them in no time . . .

Well, there must be *some* reason why none of them ever smile. It can't be the money; after all, there are only nine of them, and look at the work they get.

PART TWO

TRANSPORT AND
BUSINESS SECTION

. . . .

There are people who dismiss interest in steam trains as sentimental, or put it on the level of all non-intellectual, faintly old-fashioned and slightly immature hobbies such as fretwork, painting by numbers, or collecting beer mats.

They are people to whom one thing is the same as another thing, people incapable of perceiving form and congruence; people, above all, with no sense of grand historical peaks and watersheds, of those occasions when the past meets the future, and instead of confusion there is, for a moment, a brilliantly-articulated present, Janus-faced looking both ways. . . .

Ha! Such people will say, you cannot apply these grand historical and aesthetic perspectives to mere transport systems, the way you can to art!

Ho! I reply, you can. If it is true that Shakespeare is uniquely, unrepeatably great because in him the long slow certainties of medieval faith clash with the new questionings of the Renaissance; if Beethoven is likewise because in him the same thing happens musically, the old classical harmonies clash with the new dynamic individualism—why, then, the steam train at the height of its glory had an equally unrepeatable greatness, as the perfect formal expression of a similar balance, between a past (when people did not travel enough) and a future (when they all travel far too much).

Moreover, just as it is impossible to be certain whether Beethoven and Shakespeare were great because they perfectly represented the watershed and were thus in a sense caused by it, or because they themselves were the *creators* of the watershed, so it is impossible to be certain whether the steam train pioneers were the unconscious puppets or the conscious manipulators of enormous social forces.

For instance, they were surely taken by surprise by the fact that so many passengers wanted to use the railway, from the start—often not on commercial errands or to be at some relative's death bed, but simply for the sake of the thing. This had until then been the privilege of aristocrats only.

Railways grew from mine tramways, they were conceived by hardheaded Victorian industrialists as a quick method of moving coal and ore to factories and ports. It is symbolic that when the first railway in the world was opened on September 27, 1825, from Darlington to Stockton, the inaugural train consisted of the engine, *Locomotion*, driven by George Stephenson, tender with coal and water, six wagons with coal and passengers on top of the coal, one wagon loaded with flour and passengers, one with engineers and surveyors, a coach, *The Experiment*, for directors and their friends, which could also be used with horses on an ordinary road, six wagons of 'strangers', and finally six more wagons of coal with the passengers on top.

Just a miners' outing, really, except for a few top hats. But it was those 'strangers' who were to universalize and humanize the railway. Liberated at last from the long centuries of immobility, when only the boss-class enjoyed the luxury of personal mobility by means of the horse, which actually gave the boss-class many of its names (for what were French *chevaliers,* Spanish *caballeros,* German *ritter* or riders, English *cavaliers* or ancient Roman *equities,* gentlemen all, but horsemen?), these 'strangers' clambered on to the grimy coal wagons, demanding to be taken to far-off places, over unknown plains, under mysterious mountains to innocent seas.

In an incredibly short space of time they had caused the railway to develop a style. But this was only possible because not all the people were travelling all the time, as is the case now, with the whole world become one vast undifferentiated traffic jam. Travelling by steam train was still an event, something exciting and special, in spite of the Duke of Wellington's expressed fears in 1830 that railways were bad because 'they would encourage the lower classes to move about'.

The impression given by a French *Guide Chaix* of the 1860's, in fact, is still one of aristocratic refinement. One

72

sees people dressed as for a performance of *La Traviata*; the men with peg-top trousers, dandified waists, frock-coats in bright or pastel colours, the women in crinolines.

It is true that, leaving Paris at 6.45 a.m., they would not arrive at Marseilles till 7 a.m. the next day. It is true that, going from Aix-les-Bains to Milan (on the Chemin de Fer Victor-Emmanuel) they would have to get out of the train at St Michel to cross the Mont-Cenis pass in a horse-drawn diligence. But is not this exactly the right rhythm? To leave Paris, the Gothic north, in one misty dawn, to be subtly changed throughout the next 24 hours, coming at last to the land of red earth, olive trees, Roman amphitheatres—and to see the next dawn, brilliant, like trumpets, over that bright and classical sea!

How aware they must have been, of the vastness of the world, of its still infinite possibilities for exploration and adventure. Their journeys would have entailed just the right admixture of hardship and expense; nothing like that of doing the same thing by stagecoach, but not so little as to dull in them a delicious sense of being embarked on an enterprise. They were a world removed from today's travellers, stumbling dazed by jet-lag out of aircraft on the other side of the globe, bored, dimly aware that everything everywhere is the same.

It was not the same then. Those great expresses took you somewhere different, *other*. Very often it was to snug spas set among wooded hills, with bandstands, promenades, lakeside paths, elegant turreted little casinos and pleasure-domes winking in that lost summer light.

Writers and artists, who were to the 19th century what prophets were to the Old Testament, may have felt uneasy; 'This is what it was all leading up to,' said Henry James when World War One broke out. Lebedev, in Dostoievsky's *The Idiot,* much given to interpreting the Apocalypse, thinks the star called Wormwood means the network of railways spread all over Europe, a plague polluting the 'waters of life'. Doomed Anna Karenina meets her fatal love Vronsky on a train, and eventually dies under one.

Dickens was inspired to the famous impressionistic description of Mr Dombey's journey. 'Through the hollow, on the height, by the heath, by the orchard, by the park, by the garden, over the canal, across the river, where the sheep are feeding, where the mill is going, where the barge is floating, where the dead are lying, where the factory is smoking, where the stream is running, where the village clusters, where the great cathedral rises, where the bleak moor lies, and the wild breeze smooths or ruffles it at its inconstant will; away with a shriek, and a roar, and a rattle, and no trace to leave behind but dust and vapour, like as in the track of the remorseless monster, Death!'

But all this was just a faint cloud on the horizon of that summer sky, long before the age of mechanized slaughter. Railways may have been used strategically in the American civil war and the Franco-Prussian war, and there are indeed blurred grainy photographs of soldiers in long coats standing by huge guns on flatcars. But they never came to much. Basically steam is innocent. White puffs in a blue sky, the far-off nostalgic sound of whistles in the night, the anthropomorphic arm-motion of coupling-rods known instinctively by children all over the world.

And what style! It is assumed to be very up-to-date when a commercial organisation is styled, by highly-paid designers, right down to the buttons on the waistcoats of its doorkeepers. But there is nothing new in this, except for the high pay of the design consultants. Very early in its history the Great Western Railway of England had such things as special clothes-brushes for the use of stationmasters, with the letters GWR in dark bristles set among lighter ones; and little complimentary bottles of sal volatile, given to ladies in first-class compartments.

White tablecloths in far-off refreshment rooms, urns, antimacassars, foot-warmers, ever more elaborately interlocking timetables, fretted ironwork, curtained sleepers, wine, cigars, furs, laughter, tears, hoarse whistles in the night, utterly different landscapes of breathtaking strangeness observed on waking; the last moment in history before travel lost its magic and became a universal possession, taken for granted. They can never take that away from steam.

ONE JOURNEY FOR THE PRICE OF TWO!

It is often said that in our modern mechanised society the sense of wonder has been lost; yet few people have noticed a marvellous burgeoning of feeling for the poetry in ordinary things in, of all places, the restaurant cars of British Rail. It was *our* railways, our Spinning Jenny and the rest of the contraptions, that gave birth to the modern world, allegedly so scientific and unpoetic; but one glance at those menus will show how prophetic were Francis Thompson's lines:

> The angels keep their ancient places:—
> Turn but a stone, and start a wing!
> 'Tis ye, 'tis your estranged faces,
> That miss the many-splendoured thing.
> But (when so sad thou canst not sadder)
> Cry; — and upon thy so sore loss
> Shall shine the traffic of Jacob's ladder
> Pitched betwixt Heaven and Charing Cross.

It is perfectly true that to look at the people in restaurant cars from Charing Cross (or Euston, or Exeter, or, for that matter, even Ipswich) you would think they were stuffing perfectly ordinary food into their estranged faces: but this is probably because expense accounts have dulled their minds to the wonder of it all. To them it is just ordinary food, but British Rail know better. They are eating 'Choice Sirloin Steak with savoury butter', or 'Country Farmhouse Grill; two rashers of grilled prime back bacon, sausage, egg and tomato, with golden fried chipped potatoes'.

If they are having breakfast (with their company's £2.15) their dull eyes move unseeingly over the words 'served with your breakfast, a pot of freshly-brewed tea'. It simply does not occur to them to think of less fortunate passengers, on less glamorous lines, who merely get very old tea

75

with their breakfast, perhaps made, like that of Ernie Wise in the famous sketch about his meanness, by dipping a tea-bag on the end of a string into the water.

It means nothing to them that 'golden fried chipped potatoes' are set before them, instead of the ones coloured a kind of greasy beige and made from ground-up ceiling paper that most people get. To them it is just steak-and-chips, not a steak which has been *chosen,* by some imperious buyer in black coat and striped trousers; hundreds of steaks are laid out before him on a spotless white marble slab. 'This one,' he says, 'and this'. Suddenly he stiffens. He seizes a steak that would deceive the average housewife. His hairline moustache wrinkles fastidiously as he smells it. 'In God's name, what's *this*? Secondhand venison? Can't you see the capillaries are withered?' 'Sorry, sir,' says the obsequious butcher, 'it shan't happen again. . . .'

Not for them, either, the picture of the selected Country Farmhouses from which British Rail selects its Grills, and of course its milk (soon we shall be able to buy, I'm sure, 'your own personal disposable container of tea, with an anti-spill lid for your protection, plus sugar made from fine old Norfolk beet and an individual containerette of lustrous white Cow's Milk, plus, for your convenience, a stirrer—all this for 10p!').

'Ar,' says a gnarled old rustic leaning over the pigsty wall to scratch the ear of a Landrace gilt in pig, 'reckon you'm a-goin' to make a mort o' prime back bacon for them varmints of passingers in them ole trains, Betsy.' His ruminations are interrupted by the farm manager on his way to inspect the buxom wenches in their spotless dairy where a Fine Selection of Traditional English Cheeses is being prepared. 'Hurry up and fill that sty with fresh golden straw, Job, the British Rail buyer will be here within the hour.'

I hope, all the same, that British Rail will persevere. Maybe expense-account passengers who can afford £3.50 for just the basic lunch are beyond the reach of poetry and wonder, but I believe they could entice many of us ordinary travellers back from our cars (which even for *one* person are now cheaper than the train, let alone when the family has to be transported) if they extended this kind of prose to the whole journey.

'You will enter a world of magic the moment you leave your car in the spacious, healthy, open-air car park. For your help and information, this is not the one next to the station, which is reserved for the employees of British Rail serving you; it is located across the road, enabling you to arrive fresh at the station after a relaxing stroll of a quarter of a mile or so.'

If the station is in a large town you will find that the old style 'booking office' has been replaced by a modern Travel Centre, staffed by employees in a smart livery with striped waistcoats, who will often be seen on the platform itself (raised for your convenience from the ground level of the shining rails of best British steel to the actual level at which you enter the comfortable, walk-through carriage; you may be lucky enough to be in one of the spacious newer ones, uncluttered by old-fashioned 'arm rests', devices for opening windows, or the 'sun-blinds' with which older generations sometimes quaintly used to stop the hot sun streaming in on a very hot day).

Sometimes your ticket will be a large white card printed in vibrant scarlet; or it may be a simple, efficient piece of cardboard. Do not worry—both are equally valid! You can also buy a return ticket, if you are thinking of coming back to wherever you live. This will save you the trouble of buying another one, and to save accounting and other costs which would otherwise have to be passed on to you, the cost of this will be equal to the cost of two full single ones, not some confusing lesser sum which you might have difficulty in remembering. If you are going up, say to London, on a shopping trip, you may even buy a cheaper 'day return'; all you must remember is not to use trains at the times when you would normally go and return on an ordinary shopping trip . . .

If you are travelling from a small station you may perhaps find that there is no one in the ticket office, often a delightful old French-style guichet framed in real old Victorian wood, through which you might glimpse a delightful cosy interior with a large clock, shining old brass intruments, brown linoleum, a table laid for tea, and feel the warmth from a beautiful old stove with a roaring coke fire, although in the 'waiting room', if it does not have one side open to the weather, you may well find an electric heater placed high up in the wall where it could not set your kiddies on fire, and modern plastic seats replacing the cumbersome padded settees of yesteryear.

Here again, no need to worry! On your journey an attendant, in a smart peaked cap, will be happy to 'make out' a ticket for you, in his own personal handwriting on a special form, at no extra charge.

Once on the train, you will find everything needed to make your journey enjoyable. In addition to the luxurious restaurant car, staffed by experienced waiters in smart, stylish red jackets, there will also be a buffet car, filled with rich biscuits, delicious pieces of fruit cake especially made by British Rail's staff of aunts, streamlined cheese sandwiches in which the cheese, instead of breaking off and falling out of the sandwich in the unpredictable manner of old-fashioned 'natural' cheese, has been scientifically sliced into delicious thin sheets of uniform consistency between pre-dampened, dazzling white bread.

In the numerous toilets, each equipped with a simple device for indicating to those outside whether it is occupied or not, you will find, in addition to a real, flushing lavatory, continuous rolls of specially-chosen paper, serrated at regular intervals for easy tearing and placed within easy reach. The brilliantly-engineered wash-basins have a 'lip' to stop the water (which comes to you from *two* special taps, one hot, one cold, which you may use at the temperature of your own personal choice) from spilling over except on the most violent bends as the train swiftly bears you to your destination. And there are individual pieces of specially chosen green soap . . .

The time will pass all too swiftly, and soon you will find yourself in all the thrilling bustle of a great London station, with its continuous flow of loudspeaker announcements, its mysterious repeated calls for Mrs Oidy, passenger from Brrgong, to report to the manager's office, its snaking trains of dodgem cars laden with long rolls of carpet, rustic seats and thousands of bicycles wrapped in cardboard, clattering all over the place, its stalls offering the world's finest collection of pornographic magazines, its historic exhibitions of telephones, not connected to the Post Office system nowadays, but retained as a reminder of the days when delays in service or other causes made it necessary for passengers to use them.

THE TRAIN-WALKERS

Who are the Train-Walkers? How is it that no social commentator or historian has even noticed them, let alone studied them in depth?

Is it known, for instance, if they actually get on the train at the terminus (and, if so, is it with forged, stolen, .or somehow actually-paid-for tickets?), or do they somehow live permanently in mysterious, hidden parts of the train?

Certainly their curious activities are most in evidence for the quarters of an hour before and after the departure of the train from its starting-point. In fact I myself used to assume, thoughtlessly, that they were all people who had arrived, breathless, at the last minute, flung themselves anxiously into the last carriage, and were simply pushing their way up through the crowded rear sections, lugging their bulging bags of food and shapeless parcels and their strangely quiet children in search of seats at the front.

But, for years now, catching (to name but one) the 9.30 p.m. from Liverpool Street every Thursday evening, I have observed that this cannot be so. I notice them more on this train because I have always just spent the previous three hours rehearsing some arduous choral work. I therefore need a Guinness, and am in the crowd of regulars who instantly form the bar queue the moment we can get on, which is usually about 9.15 on the nights when

NABMSASP (National Association of Bloody-minded Signalmen and Sod the Public) are not having one of their strikes.

And, instantly, there are these Train-walkers, scrambling resolutely past, squeezing us against partitions and doors, humping ill-fastened large suitcases of faded green fabric, big sagging parcels that look as if they might contain laundry, or cartons—often bearing Japanese names—containing perhaps small washing machines, or radios that can receive and call Alaska. Sometimes they have ill-wrapped, used-looking standard lamps.

They are not breathless, indeed there is a curious faraway, glazed look in their eyes. They are *looking* for something and whatever it is, it is something on the train. If you or I get to a train in plenty of time, especially if we have a lot of stuff to carry, we naturally walk along the platform, looking in through the windows till we see some seats (and there are *always* seats on this 9.50—which is a very long train, from which various parts are detached to go to obscure silted-up ports in far, lost East Anglian marshes). We do not lug it all through the train.

Moreover, some of them are walking *from* the front of the train anyway—and it is not the same ones coming back (although they very often do later, after the train has started, still endlessly searching, passing silently through the convivial buffet car and all the other compartments).

Who are they? What are they looking for?

I believe they are the industrial equivalent of the landless labourers and dispossessed poor who wandered about England after the dissolution of the monasteries. They are the victims of the end of the First Steam Age.

Historians sometimes have to be prophets, and perhaps the more prophetic among them have already realised that, perhaps sooner than we think, a glorious Second Steam Age is coming. Steam will return. Even now, boldly encamped in the very sidings of a once-great Railway, irretrievably, to the pessimists, taken over by grinning diesel-vandals and people like NABMSASP, loyal old steam heroes are repairing the old locomotives, welding

80

new fireboxes, descaling boilers, giving their whole lives to this peaceful guerilla activity, preparing for the Day.

To the pessimist, unable to see into the future, the whole thing is like the wild, legendary, invasion-haunted period between the withdrawal of the Roman legions and the order-imposing Norman Conquest. The Railway (which sprang from Britain as Christianity sprang from Rome), incarnation of the God of Motion, inspiration of the entire modern industrial world, seems to have collapsed, we are threatened by the oil sheikhs as Spain was threatened by the Moors. We shall win, of course. Steam will return.

But there is confusion in this interim period, and the Train-walkers are one manifestation of it. They are the remnants, the refugees from the First Steam Age, when you could go from anywhere to anywhere by train, when guards were six feet tall and wore red carnations, station-masters wore top hats, porters had big turnip silver watches, railwaymen were serious, respected, moustachioed, semi-priestly, totally reliable public servants, a vast family nexus, railwaymen's sons marrying railway daughters.

Now it is all broken up, and in the chaos these Train-walkers, ex-railway people, travel ceaselessly looking for lost relatives and friends. That distant yearning in their eyes is for the lost stability of the First Steam Age. They retain a confused ancestral memory of order and a fixed way of doing things, like Amazonian natives discovered going through a strange corrupted form of the Mass in some jungle clearing 200 years after the departure of the missionaries.

All round them the ancient order has decayed. As beads, barter and local currencies replace a great national coinage, so they have seen the uniform railway ticket of yore replaced by increasingly do-it-yourself versions; over-sophistication at the centre, with tickets still retaining the authentic cardboard form and shape, issued from an enormous German machine full of winking lights, but which no one would know how to repair; under-sophistication in the wild provinces—tickets that are sometimes about the size of playing cards, sometimes paper forms printed in red, sometimes informal notes scribbled by the guard from a rough notebook when one has boarded the train at some utterly deserted station, from which the staff have all left to become outlaws in the forest (or perhaps to attend another compulsory NABMSASP meeting).

The Griddle Cars, where once, within living memory, you could get bacon and eggs, or a sophisticated steak-and-chiplet dish called a Tartan Plate, now serve only dull, cold pork pies; no one knows how to work the subtle electric hotplates.

All 'normal' rail travellers could add to the list. We just endure it, sustained by the thought of the ongoing life that still awaits us when we get off the train. But the Train-walkers are committed permanently to the Railway, forever wandering through trains, clutching their random possessions, looking for those they knew in the old days. The husband of that woman who pushes absent-mindedly through with the pale child in the thick furred anorak (though it is a warm, muggy day) may have been one of the four men laughing wildly round a table with 27 beer cans on it whom we saw on the same train yesterday. In the old days he was the Stationmaster, a respected member of the community in a neat little stone Derbyshire town, to which the nearest station is now Derby itself, 19 miles away. Now he is just Ol' George. Rumours reached her that he had been seen on the Eastern Region, she hurried down from her usual Stafford-Rugeley section, by methods known only to the Train-walkers.

They may eventually meet, they may not. Sometimes great parties of cackling women meet, the whole next carriage echoes with unintelligible jokes. For one of the indisputably sad facts about the Train-walkers is that they have lapsed into a certain gypsy roughness. In their wandering, vaguely communal life they have forgotten, for instance, that it is usual to lock the door of the lavatory. But they assume that everyone knows by instinct when they are in there; they never lock the door, so that often an unwary normal passenger, assuming the word VACANT to mean what it says, finds the door angrily slammed from inside . . .

Yet ultimately it is they who are right, they who keep alive the memory of the old days, in however confused a fashion. They know that some forms of 'progress' are a myth. They know that railways reached perfection in about 1913.

The steam power drove the wheels directly. Now we have a diesel (temporary courtesy of these sheikhs) which drives a dynamo which drives an electric motor which drives the wheels, losing heaven knows how much power on the way. In 1913 any village of any size had a station, the whole thing ran—well, not like clockwork; much better, like *steamwork*. Things like NABMSASP were just a gleam in Lenin's eye. Merely being a true, British, proper, steam Railwayman *was* the 'differential', to use today's phrase, in itself.

But it is time for the Train-walkers to wake from their seemingly hopeless dream. For it is not hopeless. Already over 300 groups or individuals own splendid, refurbished, proper steam locomotives. Some have their own lines, and uniforms with proper silver buttons, and splendid tea-rooms, and proper tickets. Let the Train-walkers alight, and join their active brothers, and lend their half-forgotten skills to the noble work of preparing for the Second Steam Age. It can't be far off now.

BRITISH RAILLERY

In spite of all those in-depth, total-breakdown-is-approaching articles, what a lot we still don't know about British railways—and I mean with a small r. Not dieselized, plastic, 'British Rail', but British railways, the first railways in the world, now in their sesquicentennial year, the first escape, over *our* misty fields, of the world's restless, swart demon-gods, hitherto pent in mines, under the earth. British, ambivalent railways, half filled with delight at the fearful energies of metal at last released, half communing with the pastoral centuries gone for ever.

Every now and then the veil is lifted. Not long ago, sitting next to a friend who teaches at Colchester Art School and who was bringing to London a large and cumbersome picture—or so it seemed in the mini-buffet car—I was enchanted when a perfectly ordinary-looking inspector, producing his excess ticket pad without batting an eyelid, wrote the amount and the words 'One Child'.

The very next day, on this same line, far from Buckinghamshire, I found screwed up in a seat corner a foolscap page of typescript, which I have since discovered was handed out to every traveller on the Marylebone-Aylesbury line. Under the plangent, Proustian title 'Autumn Timekeeping and Falling Leaves', it told a story utterly remote from the boring inter-union squabbles of mere 'British Rail', a story that instantly removes us to some deep, mysterious pre-industrial reality:

> It may seem a far-fetched excuse but your trains from Marylebone can be adversely affected by falling leaves . . . after the passage of one train the leaves are crushed to a pulp which, in certain weather conditions only, produces an extremely slippery film which is deposited on the running surface of the rail . . . a great deal of time and effort into investigating possible solutions . . . none of them has proved entirely satisfactory:
> Leaf-cleaning teams on a daily basis
> Steel brushes fitted to the train
> Train spreading detergent
> Rail-grinding train
> Sanding gear and various solutions and pastes (these had some benefit but interfered with signalling circuits).
> Electric arc mounted on the train (known as a plasma torch) and directed at the rail.
> The best hope to date lies in a special vehicle

using high pressure water sprays, which has been used effectively on BR lines in Kent where similar problems exist. LTE in conjunction with BR research Department are carrying out experiments to determine the optimum water pressure, spray nozzle shape and angle to get the best cleaning effect . . .

It also says that the problem is at its worst between Chorleywood and Chalfont.

Who could have imagined all this? Clearly they work at it right through the year, not just in autumn; and surely it is here, hidden among the mighty Chiltern beeches, that these leaf-cleaning teams (notice they put them down first) have their secret headquarters, of an earthy, dungy quality far deeper than that of the Stockbroker Tudor and Executive Country Chalet world so near yet so far from them.

This is not work for the prosaic NUR, let alone ASLEF or whatever union it is the signalmen strikers belong to. The Ancient Company of Leaf-Cleaners predate not only nationalization but all the Victorian mergers; they are older than the railway itself. They have the countryman's relationship with nature; they know it is urban folly and arrogance to think in terms of beating nature with twaddly gadgets such as 'plasma torches'. Nature is infinite, continuous, a life-process to be endlessly coped with through the recurring seasons.

They wear gaiters, leathern aprons, very dark green tweed jackets with capacious pockets, shapeless tweed hats. Their basic tool is the 'strug', a wooden pole at the end of which is a sharp metal shoe. As this is pushed along the rail, over which it fits exactly, a deft twist to the right collects the compacted leaf-mass (the 'folge', thought by some to be a corruption of 'foliage') on the right-hand spike of the shoe. Another push, and a left-hand twist completes the neat load of folge, which is then shaken off into a traditionally shaped basket known as a 'criddle'.

It looks easy, but in fact it takes years of practice. Amos

Dradgett, a Section Leaf Warden, a fine figure of a man in his middle fifties with clear, deep-set eyes in a weather-beaten face, has worked his way up from Criddle Boy, Folge Hand and Leaf-Cleaner, and is now in charge of a team which looks after 3 miles of line, known as a 'cover'.

This name derives from the Leaf-Cleaners' old tradition of invisibility to the general public. Not only a train, but any stray hiker will be the signal for a penetrating, mysteriously poignant call on the folge-horn to sound through the woods, and instantly the men, with their criddles and strugs, vanish among the trees.

This is why passengers never see them at work, let alone glimpse the carefully concealed rides up which the criddles are hauled on a continuous ropeway to a clearing in the forest, where the folge is separated into 'fireleaf', dry enough for burning on the huge, continuously smouldering, fragrant-smoking fire, and the 'drottel', which eventually becomes an immensely, magically rich compost sold only to gardeners known to the Leaf-Cleaners.

Every tea break is a picnic in this secret glade, and there is much hilarity at each new experiment of the boffins. 'What iver will they think of next, Mr Dradgett?' says a burly Leaf-Cleaner, Saul Boone. 'I heard as how that dad-gasted plasma contraption barnt roight through the rail, wholly melted it, over to Rickmansworth.'

'Har, an' I'm a-gitten nothen but a mort of sand in my criddle,' chimes in another. 'Tarnation folge ain't good for to make drottel wi' all that sand.'

'Yew don't think them scine-tists is goin' to make us what they call redandunt, dew yew, Mester Dradgett?' says Boone.

There is a deep, slow laughter in Amos Dradgett's eyes as he lights his pipe. 'Don't yew worrit, Saul boy,' he says. 'We were here afore they come, an' we'll be here arter they'm agone. They 'oont do no harm to amuse theirselves. I heerd from the brothers in Kent, yew know what they fare to do? Little ole jets o' water! My lordy, ef that don't beat all, a-gittin' up them ole wet leaves with *water*!'

The glade rings with deep-throated laughter at the absurdity of this idea. A frightful screeching sound, setting everyone's teeth on edge, comes near, rises to a climax, dies away. Peering from their cover, they see the latest attempt, the 'rail-grinding train'. Amos wrinkles his brow, then brightens.

'That'll be steel filin's in the drottel now; but us can manage. Goo yew down the warkshop, Saul, an' bring me a parful magnit. They ain't goin' to beat us ole Leaf-Cleaners yet . . .'

THINGS AIN'T WHAT THEY USED TO BE

British railways are not like other railways. Fundamentally they are mine tramways. Trevithick and Stephenson both came from a background of mines and mining. Coal, iron, *things,* never mind about people.

Things have a much better time of it. A crowd of commuters stands, wet and shivering, on the platform, when there is a click in the loudspeakers, then an announcement: 'Grerksqxx krkk the hai naw nee do lunn runna box ditty dirty binny day.' While the more experienced travellers are working out that this means: 'The 8.14 to London is running approximately 30 minutes late,' (they always say approximately, never just about), a train of huge identical containers thunders through, blam, blam, blam, at 90 m.p.h.

When the people's train does come, the deeper in commuter-land, the older the carriages are likely to be. Often the fittings seem to have been doled out grudgingly like workhouse furniture in the 19th century:—

Long seats, covered with gloomy maroon or dust-coloured fabric	2
Mirror	nil
Ashtrays in smoking compartment to seat 6 each side	1
Springs	nil

Stylized map of network (since dratted fools of
   passengers are always wanting to know
   where they are and where to get out)   1

Actual staff are always kind and helpful. It's these thing-obsessed bosses who set the tone (and why did not they put up a better fight, merely on a freight basis, against the Beeching cuts, seen to be barmier year by year as ever-bigger industrial circus-trains take to the roads?).

There are, it is true, the excellent Inter-City services, but already the return fare to Preston from Euston is £20 second, £28 first. The fact is, passenger trains are going to get either older and older till all commuters use cars, or faster, more luxurious, dearer and progressively less realistic until there is only one left. It will go at 200 m.p.h. be equipped with secretaries, couriers, manicurists, masseuses, swimming pool, turkish bath, cinema and 12-piece orchestra, and will be ready to go to any destination desired by the sole passenger, Mr Ravi Tikkoo or the Aga Khan.

The further a train is going, the higher the proportion of first-class carriages. The second-class are invariably walk-through ones; none of your cosy, semi-detached private compartments for the peasants. They are not going to truckle to the second-class populace if they can help it. They pursued right to the inside of Holloway Prison Mrs Melville, a commuter from Brighton. Her offence was that, sitting in a first-class carriage because all the second were full as usual, she agreed to pay the difference between second and first but not the *whole* first, as demanded.

They want to phase us all out. First the commuters, then the second-class and finally even the first-class, so that they can get back to carrying *things*. The old, the real Euston was approached through a splendid monument like the Arc de Triomphe. Until it was pulled down by puny wretches it did indeed celebrate the vast triumph of Victorian railway buildings—all those embankments and tunnels, and viaducts and fretwork stations, connecting London with Liverpool, Manchester, Glasgow, far-off Scottish moors; Beattock, Aberdeen, Inverness. But it was also *human*. It was full of nooks and corners, and funny little rooms, and horsehair sofas, and statues, and potted palms, and old photographs and war memorials.

It was threaded and interfused by teeming, various, Dickensian life. You could have a bath or get your hair cut or have a snack in a spacious bar with friendly hissing urns, or have a grand meal with waiters under a high classical ceiling. In fact you could *live* there if you wanted because there was a hotel as well.

There is no hotel at the new Euston. There is not even a waiting room, as such. There is simply this architect's-drawing stark hall, which looks as though a giant with a huge dust-pan had impatiently swept every fidgety human requirement—the shops, tea, the pornography stall, the chemist's, the lavatories, the ticket windows, every-thing—into the sides, all cramped up against one another, all too small.

If you are lucky enough to find one of the mingy plastic seats, within 30 seconds an Indian with a long brush will come round sweeping litter from round and under it. They made the floor of some fancy dark material, not realising that every toffee paper, crumb and orange pip would be blindingly, inescapably visible. There must have been plenty of litter at the old, the real Euston, but it simply was not noticed, it was part of the comfortable human scene. It certainly was not necesesary to have full-time men going round incessantly pouncing on every speck of paper the moment it appeared, like neurotic housewives.

At the new Euston they do not let the dratted passengers see the trains at all until they are let on to the platform for the long walk. At other main-line stations, older and more traditional, they are compelled to let the people mill about among the trains. But only at their peril, because all the railwaymen, absorbed, withdrawn, secret, ignoring the people, are furiously driving smaller trains of their own about the platforms.

As soon as there is any group or queue of passengers they drive straight at it, with angry little peep-peeps. Behind them, clanking and wobbling, is a long snake of 23

89

trolleys with high sides of wire mesh. These trolleys are laden with extraordinary piles of rustic seats, bicycles, lawn-mowers, long rolls of carpet, dustbins . . .

Things, all things. More and more the railwaymen look at passengers with an air of faint surprise, as if to say, 'Oh, are you still there?' Sometimes they do not even bother to collect the tickets. Nobody comes round on the train and there is nobody about at the other end of the journey. At other times ticket inspectors, sometimes one after the other and sometimes all together, laughing secretly among themselves, come through the train.

What are they laughing at?

The train stops for a mysterious 12 minutes, just 500 yards outside the London terminus. The passengers anxiously consult appointment diaries, watches, air tickets with reporting times written in blue carbon. When they finally do arrive the loudspeakers are saying, 'OLOGISE FOR THE LATE A BY HEE JARRY A WOIN IN NOPE A NOY SQUERKLE.' People run for buses, tubes, taxis and ha ha ha, ask taximen what they think about the new Euston; *peep peep peep,* watch it, do not get run over by another load of carpet, rustic seats and dustbins. OLOGISE FOR THE WEEOW A DULY BOILY WASHAM HAW HEE DUE TO A SNAILY BUCKET AT THRINGLE . . .

The four ticket inspectors walk slowly away, still laughing among themselves. *What are they laughing at*? A terrible thought strikes me. They are thinking, perhaps, about the day when they get *us* inside those containers.

SHAMBLES AND NEATPOTS

In the last 20 years or so, life has got progressively more orientated towards Neatpots and against Shamblers. This is very confusing because very few people are complete Neatpots—totally organised, finicky, dexterous, tidy, obedient, disciplined, their desks (if they are desk people) clear at the end of each day; and every few are complete

Shamblers, setting off on random journeys, wearing odd socks, forgetting to put their clocks back or forward, losing tickets, unable to fold a newspaper in a crowded train—and, of course, having chaotic desks.

Most normal people oscillate between these two poles. The pressures of life force them into an increasingly Shambler attitude, then one day the Neatpot side ups and says 'enough of this'. They clear their desks, they sew up the hole in the coat lining where the ticket keeps slipping through, they even get all that ghastly rubbish of sweet papers, odd gloves, forlorn little springs, Band-aids, crayons and small foreign coins from under the back seat of the car.

But the tendency now is to try and suppress all trace of the Shamblers and to make public life 100 per cent Neatpot. The new Euston station (opened in 1968) is a classical example. The old Euston was a marvellous reminder that there is nothing necessarily inefficient about Shamblers; it was a great Victorian monument to Shamblers, and the Victorians were a damn sight more efficient than we are.

They built that great rambling, Shambling, station, which instantly became a place bursting with teeming, unselfconscious human life. It had a sense of occasion, of mystery, of the beginning and ending of fateful journeys, for was there not a great Greek ceremonial arch? But roads, ordinary human roads, went right in among the railway lines; the hissing locomotives came practically into a hotel dining room with wicker chairs and palms; on Platform 14 there were mysterious *bathrooms,* with polished brass taps, where you could have a bath after getting in from Scotland. There was a huge waiting room with horsehair sofas and an upper gallery, as in some Renaissance church, with doors that may have led to offices or to chapels; it would not have been surprising if processions of boys had issued forth in white surplices singing Palestrina. Nor would it have been surprising if Dickensian brawls and scuffles, drunken fights, had broken out (indeed, since Euston serves Scotland and

Ireland, they often did). There were strange hidden little Refreshment Rooms with people that seemed to *live* there, never actually catching, trains, just drinking port, or still green lemonade, and eating buns. There was, of course, a Tea Room. It was a Shambler's Paradise.

Look at it now. A Neatpot sarcophagus, built of some substance that seems to repel human life as oil repels water. Indeed it does not take much imagination to see it, in one of those gloomy the-future-will-be-hell films, as a kind of euthanasia centre; to slightly louder Muzak than there is now, all Shamblers over 60 will be ushered by uniformed attendants on to trains from which there is no return. . . .

It is no good going to the new Euston with a Shambler family clutching oranges and brown paper bags of bodgy sandwiches—especially if the Neatpot side of your character has caused you to come in good time and there is nothing to do but wait. The 12 plastic seats (no benches; suppose some Shambler came and actually wanted to lie down!) will already be occupied by refugees from some huge varicose veins outpatients department. Solemn Neatpot men with briefcases and no imaginable family will stare resentfully at your scruffy children, dropping sweet papers visible on the black floor from 20 yards to an old Tamil with a long brush and dust-pan, himself sadly aware of being a Shambler working for Neatpots, who will promptly come and sweep them up.

(No, stay, those Neatpot men do not have 'no imaginable family'. They have, in fact, 1.87 children each, and live in executive-type chalets with wall-to-wall carpeting, a carport, and a hi-fi with 49.7 LPs of Frank Sinatra, and are the Average Reader and Average Viewer that most editors, all advertising managers and all TV producers dream about.)

If you want to telephone at Euston or anywhere else, instead of a nice big black telephone with a flexible lead, in a kiosk, and a Button B that gives your money back if you do anything wrong, there will now be this fragile off-beige Neatpot STD thing, on a semi-rigid lead that makes it quite difficult for you to replace the handset so that it will lie down properly. When the pip-pips start this will be just too soon for you to be able to tell whether the voice they have cut short at the other end is the one you want. Unless you instantly find the critical angle, allowing less deviation than that at which a spacecraft must re-enter the earth's atmosphere, at which you have to push in the 10p, it will go in just after the pip-pips have stopped, and there is no way of getting it back. No good bothering with a 2p unless the person is near enough for you to drop in on personally anyway; it will cut you off in your third sentence. You won't be in a kiosk, either; just an open-ended Perspex acoustic helmet, so that people can steal the bag from under your feet while you try to telephone.

It goes without saying that all new office buildings are Neatpot, a fact which becomes all the more obvious when you see the obstinately Shambler paper decorations which appear in them every Christmas—although of course with every Christmas there are increasing efforts to make us buy spiky Neatpot ones, little dry glittering plastic frosty Christmas trees which won't scatter all those Shambler pine needles on the carpet, and which will naturally be lit by Neatpot Electric Merrilites, not by Shambler candles.

Since there is in all normal people a natural, almost gravitational slide towards Shambling (whereas it requires the opposite, a kind of vertical, conscious re-tensioning, to become and remain Neatpot), Neatpot buildings can sometimes, in spite of themselves, take on a slightly Shambler aspect. The Royal Festival Hall, on a good night, can be quite jolly, especially when the people have come to hear a real Shambler composer like Brahms or Elgar. Theoretically the Hovercraft, too, is a Neatpot vehicle, whizzing efficiently over to France in 50 minutes; but somehow the laughing holiday family parties turn it into something almost as Shambler as a real boat.

Theoretically, also, some Neatpot developments benefit everyone, including Shamblers. Anyone, for instance, must find a bank credit card useful if he runs out of cash in a strange town (although curiously enough the process of getting a new cheque book is *more* Shambler than it used to be, now that you have to do all that printing in capitals for them). Trouble is, the Shambler loses his credit card (or, at the very least, has to go through all the contortions of feeling through the hole in the lining of his inside pocket down to the bottom of his jacket, while the Neatpot customers in the bank stare at him). Neatpots have folding scissors that can open those plastic bags of sweets at garages, Shamblers have to tear them open with their teeth.

The new Underground ticket machines, and those turnstile slots that make as if to gobble your finger, are aggressively Neatpot. The Neatpot ball-point has totally displaced the Shambler pen or pencil (the best Shambler pencil is a 4B; if Neatpots ever use pencils they have thin hard Hs). Steam was Shambler, diesel is Neatpot. Almost all car manufacturers have stopped making Shambler convertibles and turn out saloons more Neatpot, more sealed and shut-in, with every year. We have Neatpot decimal currency, and they are now trying to sell us Neatpot digital clocks and watches, as if there could be *any* improvement on the instant, comfortable visual recognition of the hands we have known since the earliest Shambler grandfather clocks. And who ever heard of a Shambler Computer; the ultimate contradiction?

All the same, I don't think the Neatpots are going to have it all their own way. When we old Shamblers feel oppressed and in need of comfort we have only to look at the way the young dress.

POST HASTE

Practically everyone's reaction to that news item about the new Post Office service in Brighton guaranteeing to deliver a letter on the day it is posted, for the astounding fee, even these days, of 60p, must have been to wonder who would use this method in preference to sending the message by a train of camels, or a man on horseback, or even the telephone.

If they guaranteed to get it to, say, New York, or even just Altnaharra (Sutherland) on the same day, there might be some point in it. But it only operates within a '12-mile coastal strip'.

Why *this* coastal strip? First reports tell vaguely of 'lawyers, doctors and estate agents' using the service. But such people, surely, are the core of the telephoning classes?

Obviously they are not in Brighton. One can only conclude that, unnoticed, or skilfully concealed, among the commuter and holiday bustle of 'London-by-the-sea' there still survives an intense, exclusive 18th-century fashionable life, full of affignments, invitations to routs and affemblies and écarté parties, duels, perhaps even meffages to French men-o'-war lying off Beachy Head, which has gone on since the place was called Brighthelmstone, before even the Prince Regent discovered it.

The handsome, erect, grey-haired woman locks up her antique shop in the Lanes. After an anxious look round, as though for an expected visitor, she shrugs angrily and turns towards Hove. She is Lady Amalia Westonhaugh, and is giving a small ball in her rooms tonight for her ward Dorothea d'Eynville. She is angry because Dumbleton, the carrier, has not arrived with his cart to transport her best harpsichord from the shop to her house, although she had sent the letter to him this morning by her aged footman and messenger, Tomkins.

She had also sent out the embossed invitations, by the same method, this morning, only deciding to give the ball because the previous day her friend Lady Marchmont had sent, by *her* aged footman Perkins, a note apprising her that Sir Gresham Fulke's son, Toby, had that day come back from his plantations, 'and although Dorothea is sweetly pretty, there are so many forward minxes in the Town that I know you will want to lose no time, so I am sending you this by Perkins'.

'Ods, ma'am, 'twas a fortunate chance I was passing in this demned rainy weather.' A voice hails her from an elegant post-chaise. ''Tis a plague on me gout, and I'll warrant no good for that fine Paris gros-grain mantle of yours neither!'

'La, Sir Julius, we are well met. I am vastly obliged to you.' Lady Amalia bites her lip; Sir Julius is the last person she wanted to meet. He and his foppish son Anthony were not among those to whom Tomkins had taken invitations. Now she must pretend this was an error, since Sir Julius will surely see the preparations at her house.

'Egad, 'tis a trifle, ma'am. My man Hodgkin shall set off at once and deliver the message to Dumbleton, if ye'll be so kind as to entrust him with the keys of your shop.'

She does not know that Sir Julius, that very afternoon, had been handed a sealed envelope by Bunnion, the old footman of the devious lawyer Silas Dring:

'My dear Sir Julius: A foot-servant from an Estate Agent whom I do not need to name to you has this morning brought me a letter confirming that the Bank are about to foreclose on the Mortgage of Lady W's Shop. I trust this information will be to our mutual Benefit. Kindly burn this upon receipt. Ever Yr. Obdt. Servt. S. Dring.'

In vast good humour, Sir Julius had given the panting Bunnion half a sovereign. 'There's for thy pains, my good man. You seem in a taking.'

'Ah, thankee kindly, Sir. Aye, a mort of running I've done for Master Dring today! A letter to Lady Weston-haugh, and another to a gentleman over in Rottingdean.' (That old scoundrel Dring in touch with the smugglers as well, Sir Julius thought.)

At Lady Westonhaugh's, Sarah, the old housekeeper, is putting up Miss Dorothea's hair with hot crimbling-irons. 'I beseech you, Miss, hold still, or I shall burn your pretty neck, as had all the fine gentleman admiring it at Sir Joshua's rout in the Pavilion, they tell me.'

Lady Westonhaugh enters, looking distraught, with a letter just brought by old Johnson, foot-servant to kindly Dr Pauncefoote, who has long loved her from afar:

'My dear Lady Westonhaugh; I returned from some

96

visits in Kemp Town, where there are some sad cases of Rising of the Lights, Headmouldshot, and the Purples, to find yr. man, Tomkins, with yr. kind Invitation. The poor old fellow was in a sad state of the Palsies, so I have taken the liberty of putting him to bed here, after applying a cataplasm and bleeding him. My man Johnson shall deliver the rest of yr. Communications, and will then arrive with this one, I trust not too late to inconvenience you, for he, too, is advanced in years, and I have advised him not to over-exert himself. Permit me to subscribe myself, Yr. Ever-respectful Admirer, R. Pauncefoote.'

'Interfering old fool!' says Lady Westonhaugh angrily. 'Who will mix the negus now?'

'Faith, ma'am,' says Dorothea, 'you do him an injustice. I wish you had cared for him more than for that horrid Sir Julius. And, as for the messages, he is quite right. It is all becoming too much for these old servants, who will never be replaced. Why cannot we use the telephone, like anyone else?'

'La, Miss,' says Sarah, 'I couldn't abide one of them nasty things in the house, giving us all electrical shocks.'

'You know not what you are saying, child,' says Lady Westonhaugh. 'I think only of your good. Toby Fulke—'

'Foh! 'Tis a prancing coxcomb! I think nothing of him' says Dorothea stamping her foot pettishly.

As a matter of fact, with the ungratefulness of youth, she has plans to telephone Rick Deadbeat, leader of a group called The Sausage doing a one-night gig at the Pier Ballroom, and elope with him this very night . . .

But for the rest of them this new Post Office service has obviously come in the nick of time.

I'D LIKE A CADILLAC, IF YOU HAVEN'T GOT ONE

We may as well admit it. The motor car is becoming less and less a functional object with every day that passes, more and more of a waiting-room on wheels. It becomes more and more difficult to allow the car its proper function, that of moving, and often more difficult even than that to find anywhere to put it when it has stopped moving. I cherish the memory of a cartoon film in which some character had a car which he could not park, so he folded it in half, then in half again, and again, until it was just a little thing he popped into his briefcase, with which he then disappeared into some city building.

We cannot go as far as that, but there is a lot to be said for easing the social stress of this non-functionality of the car, taking the curse off it, indeed rationalising the non-carness of cars today, by making them purely static art objects, like the wooden aeroplanes of the Polynesian cargo cults (with which the islanders hope to procure a magic rain of 20th-century blessings) or even by making purely disposable cars, perhaps of cake, or sugar, or liquorice, which could afterwards be ceremonially eaten.

There are probably many younger readers who have no notion of what it was like in the heyday of cars, their functional golden youth. I shall come back to cake cars in a minute. For a moment just let me bathe in the nostalgia behind some words I jotted down in a notebook on the wide, new, triple-carriageway A12 one Saturday morning, as I sat there in the queue, with the engine actually switched off (must see about that slow-running jet). The words I jotted down were *bull-nose, hot leather, wd. like Cadillac if you not got one.*

I am just old enough to remember the days when the motor car had any practical use, let alone being a possession that gave *pleasure.* True, I got a whiff of it, not being born into the class that bowled in Hispano-Suizas or Isotta-Fraschinis down empty poplar-lined roads to shimmering southern seas, or, in those Bentleys with four pieces of vacuum-cleaner hosing coming out of the bonnet on each side, turned from London towards secret mansions or great windy moors ('Adèle's gloved hand rested lightly on the wheel as the great car swung north . . .'). We never owned a car at all, in fact; but my father, even when unemployed in the Depression, would usually manage to buy a great old bull-nose Morris for £5 in August, trundle us round bed-and-breakfasts in North Wales for a few days, and then sell it for £6.

In this big old tourer (the word *convertible* not yet having been imported), with its high leather seats and great bare wooden dashboard containing a brass speedometer (I can smell that leather now, under a rare hot Welsh sun), and a lever on the steering column for *retarding the ignition,* he would start the holiday journey with a wide detour out of Coventry so that we could drive past the station where queues of people humping bags and suitcases were waiting for crowded trains.

The only time I have had a feeling of comparable joy as a driver myself was during the petrol rationing after Suez (remember?). I stayed working quietly at home, then blew all the coupons in one glorious, utterly unchecked run to London. Bowling through the little white clapboard Essex villages, through which the narrow, pre-bypass A12 wound, I felt as though I were living in some Wells fantasy and had slipped into a previous century, astonishing the people with my marvellous horseless carriage. I half expected them to attack me with pitchforks, or else carry me off to be their king. And in London itself, what ease of parking, what spacious cross-city journeys! It was like driving in the early morning when nobody is about . . . only of course there were lots of people about, and the splendid thing was that they were all on foot except me.

This may not say much for human nature (or my nature anyway). But it is an iron logic that the more cars there are, the less they can fulfil this primary function of giving you perfect, mobile freedom. And, paradoxically, those high roomy old cars, with no pretensions to aerodynamic styling (indeed an aspidistra in the back would not have looked really out of place) would fit the conditions of modern urban driving very much better than those low-slung, wicked-looking *fastbacks,* really only at home on Daytona Beach or the Utah Salt Flats. What we need is more slowbacks.

That is one of the two ways in which we could come to terms with the idea of the non-moving or, to coin a useful word, immotor car. Instead of the few random accessories now available, such as Travelling Scrabble and, of course, radios, which at least take note of the fact that there are long periods when a driver is not driving, we should very much enlarge this idea of the car as an alternative house. I do not mean in the literal, *caravan* sense (that is a separate issue; people with caravans have this special view of life as something that happens in a sloping field where there are 249 other caravans, all white, cream, or a particularly bilious green). I mean just ordinary cars.

Why are there so few things to *do* in cars? If their dimensions were re-thought on the spacious lines of the old bull-nose Morris, they could contain small workbenches, stoves, desks, sewing-machines, bookshelves. There could be chest expanders, rowing machines or bicycle exercisers—a special neat motoring variety, bearing the same relation to the ones you see in a gymnasium as those car vacuum cleaners do to real domestic ones. I myself would like to have a piano; in fact a nice throbbing traffic jam would be a very good place for practising, because you wouldn't be disturbing the neighbours—not permanent neighbours anyway.

But this would be an intermediate stage, while the mass of the people still held to the idea of a car as something that would *eventually* get them somewhere, even along the North Circular Road. But the final stage would involve total acceptance, by people in an oil-less 2000 AD, that actually to *go* anywhere would involve the use either of feet, bicycle, horse or electric train, while at the same time recognising that the car as such is a thing, a shape, an object with *mana,* semi-sacred, a kind of 20th-century corn dolly, that will be with us for ever.

In fact corn dollies are already made in such shapes as Man in Armour, Cornucopia, Cambridgeshire Umbrella, so it is about time the practitioners of this revivified art turned to making something more relevant to our time, corn dolly cars; little ones to hang in the hall, full-size ones to go in the garage. People could spend their weekends dusting these, instead of (as in many cases even now)

100

polishing them. For those who preferred the old-fashioned polishing there could be quite cheap disposable ones, made of polishable foil moulded over a light plastic framework, guaranteed to last say a dozen polishings, after which a new one could be bought. About £7.50, they would cost. Or, of course, plastic cars, made of a substance that you could have melted down and moulded into a different 'model'.

You could have cars made of candle-fat too, obviously with a vast wick, guaranteed to burn 200 hours; a practical gift. There would be chocolate cars too, of course, and cars made of liquorice or bread or icing sugar, or for the man who has everything, full size glass Rolls-Royce filled with wine. Everywhere the basic, magic shape of the car would be maintained, satisfying our obscure and insatiable need for it, and without the dreadful frustration of trying to move in it. How happy we should all be—especially me, with all those lovely empty roads stretching invitingly before my fastback.

CAR FOR *WHAT* FAMILY?

I somethimes wonder if any motoring correspondents are married, let alone fathers of families. Time and again I see on a motoring page some such headlines as J. R. GOODWHEEL (or HAROLD TWEEDCOAT or MONTY CARLOW)TESTS A NEW FAMILY 2/LITRE. And what do I find? Absolutely nothing about its family aspect at all. They seem to me to have joined a conspiracy with the manufacturers to ignore the fact that where there are family saloons there are, more often than not, children. That's what a family *is*; father, mother and children, not necessarily in that order.

Quite often there's a picture of the motoring correspondent, usually wearing some kind of smart cap or woolly hat. And either he's alone in the car, or he has some dolly bird with him in the front seat. His article is all about torque, and compression ratio, and something called understeer. Sometimes one of his mild complaints is about the difficulty of hearing the soft, low voice of the dolly bird in the wind noise or vibration that occurs around the 85 m.p.h. mark, in spite of the improved windscreen angle.

Gosh, in our family saloon nobody with a soft, low voice would stand a chance, at *any* speed. What I'd like to read about is the sound-proofing, because any outing we have is a shouting as well—especially towards the end of the day, when the past 20 miles have been too much for them and they start pinching each other. Once, near the end of a long journey, I was startled by an unusually loud scream from the back. I braked sharply and pulled in to the side, and I was shouting at them when I realised that someone was shouting at *me* from outside.

It was a police motor-cyclist. 'Why didn't you give a signal?' he yelled above the din. 'I nearly ran into you.'

It shut them up as I never could have. But it set me wondering, not for the first time, why my so-called family saloon doesn't have a few family features, such as sound-absorbent lining material.

Ideally, this scream-absorbent but easily wipeable material would also (unlike linoleum) be very flexible. This would enable the body trimmers to fit it across the cracks through which, at present, fantastic amounts of rubbish get into the spaces under the rear seats. They're quite small cracks, but you wouldn't believe what gets through them; every month I clear out odd socks, cardboard dominoes stuck together with sweets, comics, gloves, plastic men, boats, halves of scissors, dolls, furry apple cores, gumboots, toy dustpans, jigsaw pieces and small rubber octopuses.

Mention of wiping down brings me to an obvious need in any family saloon—somewhere to put the damp cloth. Actually we always carry two damp cloths, one for sticky hands and faces, one for sticky bits of car (they have de-misters, why can't they have de-stickifiers?).

These damp cloths are part of something the manufacturers (and their stooges the correspondents) don't seem to have heard about; in-car luggage. They seem to think you can put everything in the boot except, for some reason gloves. They provide this little hole (felt-lined usually, and utterly unwipeable), often with a lid that keeps falling down after you've had the car for three months, which they actually call the *glove-box*.

It's one of the things the motoring correspondents like to mention, along with the understeer and the grouping of the instruments. 'I liked the roomy glove box,' they say.

Who the devil has roomy gloves, or any kind of gloves, when they're driving a family car? Our glove-box is full of sweet papers, bits of an old torch in which the battery has started to exude a peculiarly sticky yellow paste, and torn fragments of maps.

There certainly isn't room for in-car luggage there. For us (and I suspect for many travelling families) the in-car luggage goes in a large shopping-bag (ours is known as the *bulgy-bag*) which keeps falling against my wife's legs every time we go round a corner, unless she moves it and it falls against *my* legs. There's absolutely nowhere to put it, but it's vital on a long journey, being crammed with sandwiches, wire puzzles, nappies, cardboard cups, biscuits, apples, chocolate, rag books. plastic baubles, crayons and various medicines.

Then of course there are the bottles. I've got a 4-litre family saloon, but it's four litres of milk. No real family goes more than ten miles without a minimum of three bottles, containing milk, soft drinks, and water. The water is often used for making more soft drinks and for keeping the damp cloths damp, and the damp cloths are often used for mopping up milk or soft drinks that have been spilt, over my wife's legs or mine, when we go round a corner. The thing, as you see, is self-perpetuating.

But I've never seen a family saloon that gives you somewhere to put all these bottles. In fact the whole question of eating and drinking has been disregarded. If the manufacturers had cared to ask me, I could have told them that the more children you have the more often you have to stop to drink (let alone anything else) because they all get thirsty at different times.

This necessitates a great deal of drinking, and of course eating, in the car because very often it is raining. It's a funny thing, but the more it rains, the thirstier and the hungrier they get. But there is no flat surface anywhere in the so-called family saloon on which to put a cup of anything.

Why can't they have little trays, like the ones on the backs of aircraft seats, instead of those footling ashtrays which inquisitive little fingers wrench out in the first mile? (And what kind of family do they think I've got anyway, all smoking away in the back there?)

So there you are, correspondents. The ideal family saloon that I want to read about will have these features:

1. Scream-absorbent interior trim, but easily wiped down.
2. Larder and bottle store.
3. Flat surfaces for drinking, eating, jigsaws, etc.
4. No controls, even those for winding down windows, operable unless ignition switched on.
5. De-stickifiers, pencil sharpeners and non-return rubbish receptacles as standard equipment.
6. Front seats fixed to floor with immense rigidity (so occupants cannot feel them being pushed by knees or feet from behind).
7. Reserve periscopic mirror system so that when child in the back has its feet pressed against the roof (yes, the *roof*) driver can still see traffic behind.
8. Assortment of interesting-looking knobs and levers that can be pulled, wrenched and detached but are really dummies.
9. Air supply for blowing up balloons.
10. Either seats on to which those hook-over baby-holders actually fit, or let the people who make hook-over baby-holders go and have a look at existing family saloons.

Let the industry make a start with these, and *then* I might start reading about the in-line, cross-flow engine, the

104

McPherson strut dampers, the convenient map-reading light, the understeer and the rest of it. At least I'll have finished the journey fresh enough to try.

LORRY LYRIC

Lorry, lorry, lorry. Car. Another lorry.
  Lorry, lorry, me. Another lorry. Sorry,
Lorry men from Beccles, Bootle, Bray, and Barry,
  Bury, Brum. I know what useful loads you carry,
Containers, cumbrous-cubic, carting cornflakes, curry,
  Chairs and cheese and steel and stone and quarry
     slurry;
Lathes and lamps and biscuits, beer and boots you
     ferry . . .
  But, lorry, lorry, lorry! England's far from
     merry,
Dreary and not cheery, and very weary, very.
  Is the bleary eye all blurry of the driver in
     a hurry
Who must tarry, never scurry, in this sorry lorry
     flurry
  Or his horror hara-kiri will harrow up a jury
In Jarrow, or in Surrey. O the folly! O the fury!
  The one thing I would like to know
Is where do all these lorries GO?
  Concatenated car-transporters clank
(Their eight rear wheels oft skim the bank
  Of B-road hemmed by hedge and stile
With ten straight yards in every mile)
  Quite empty, though it's plain to see
They're going OUT from Coventry
  Or else (this lorry thing all over!)
Taking Fiats INTO Dover.
  Is it just me, or is it true
All Yeovil people ever do
  Is send their furniture up north?
This huge high nodding van's the fourth

105

From Yeovil I have passsed today
On straight but narrow (damn!) Fosse Way.
    And who the hell on one day sent
A thousand tons of wet cement
    Churned and chomped as it goes along
In conical convoys fifty strong?
What crazed consortium-board of bankers
Financed this uncountable tide of tankers
Sloshing with chemicals, oil and grain
Down MY short cut, MY secret lane?
    And when I escape to a Major Road
Wouldn't you know—an accurst Wide Load.
    An enormous cylindrical iron Thing
Taking two hours from Thame to Tring
    In a crawling queue reaching out of sight.
(Why can't they move these Things at night?) . . .
A lyric on lorries, I'm sad to say
And sorry, O lorries, must end this way
    Must end on a plaintive note, beseeching
Couldn't they SEE this would follow Beeching?

SPRING SONG

'Even little-used country lanes off the beaten track were
being explored by many family motorists. Many with
young children went for walks in woodlands and down
leafy lanes picking posies of wild primroses for Mothering
Sunday . . . road patrols were inundated with calls for
help, mainly because of overheating and gearbox trouble.'
                    RAC announcement

Spring, the sweete Spring, is the year's pleasant king
When wee goe out to the woodes neare Tring,
Hey ding-a-ding ding
Hey clang-a-bang clank, with a Tyger in the tank
Sweet motorists love the Spring!

Spring, the sweete Spring, when the birds do wing!
Wee got as far as Esher as quicke as anythinge—

Hey! Jug-a-jug noise! Hey,clatter-clatter too!
Hey nonny—in the bonnet, look, steam coming
  through!
Sweet motorists love the Spring!

Spring, the sweete Spring! With my love I took a
  drive
And the brake fluid failed, in a Hillman '55
So ring-a-ring ring
The patrolman did bringe
And he did twitter 'Whoo! It's a wonder you're alive!'
Sweet lovers love the Spring!

Spring, the sweete Spring! Well, once my love and I
Meant to go to Brighton, but in a lay-bye
Hey ding-a-ding bong, there was something very wronge
In the clutche (or the geare-box, never ask me why,
And I'd just had the bill for a new front wing)
Sweete lovers love the Spring!

Spring, the sweete Spring! In my youth and my pride
I bought a new car and I took my love a ride;
Hey ding-a-ding ding, to mee did she cling.
In a lane in the Chilterns I gave my love a ring
In the car which soon, white-ribboned, would bear her
  as a bride;
Sweet lovers love the Spring!

Spring, the sweete Spring! Now my car is second-
  hand
And the queue to the countrie each week-end doth
  expand;
In Spring, the sweete Spring, we packed sandwiches
  of ham
And missed the turne at Barnet in a nose-to-bumper
  jam
While the children in the back
Had gobbled all the snack
For the pic-nicke in the woodland, by the river, as
  we planned.
Hey ding-a-ding! Child,

107

I thought *this* was the wood where the flowers grew
 wild
But let's hurry back, for I fear very much
That something really terrible has happened to the
 clutche;
Hey ring-a-ring road, we shall end up being towed
And this is the moment when I'm trying not to sing
Some motorists *hate* the Spring.

MAN IN THE MIDDLE

I'm a perfectly ordinary, normal motorist. Never had a neurosis in my life. Happily married, fine kids, reasonable job. Car two-and-a-half years old and sound as a bell.

But the more I drive these days the harder it is not to believe I am being followed. And preceded. Always by the same two men; the Man Behind and the Man in Front.

The Man Behind is, to put it plainly, an arrogant, reckless young idiot. And I don't say this because he has a newer and more powerful car than mine. I'm perfectly ready to let him pass when conditions are safe. I'm not one of those fellows you read about who feel their virility is challenged when someone passes them. As I said, I've got these fine kids. How many has this Julian got?

I'm sure he has some name like that. You don't get a car like that at his age unless you're some rich young fool with more money than sense.

Either that, or he's the youngish, jumped-up manager of some faintly shady company. It's the company's car, that's why he takes these risks with it. He wouldn't throw it about like that if he had been through the deposit-and-instalment mill like the ordinary motorist, like me.

Ha, now we're coming up to some red traffic lights, he's trying to creep up level with me on the inside lane. Oh no you don't Nigel. I'm not such a fool as that. Obviously it's up to me, on behalf of the great silent majority of normal motorists, to teach him a lesson by moving smartly back in. Hasn't he got the intelligence anyway to see that I wasn't out there on the crown of the road just to spite him? Can't he see I was waiting for a chance to get past the dunderheaded old fool, the Man in Front (more of him in a moment)?

I may be an ordinary humdrum motorist but that doesn't mean I've got slow reactions. As a matter of fact I've got rather quick reactions. I'm not one of these chaps you see fumbling with the gears after the lights have gone to green. See, the moment they turn to amber I—

—now look, Bruce, it's no good sounding your horn at me like that. If there's one thing that irritates the ordinary motorist it is this kind of implication that he has gone to sleep. I rather pride myself on my getaway. I'd like to see young Lochinvar here do it any better with this car. He'll be flashing his headlights at me next—

—oh, *go* on then, get on with it and break your neck. He wouldn't have got past me and the Man In Front if he hadn't got a car with acceleration like that, I can tell him.

Well, at least I don't have to worry about him any more. I can devote all my attention to the Man In Front—and heaven knows I need to. If this didn't happen to be Thursday I should dismiss him as a weekend driver. But he's right there in front of me, every day of the week.

He seems to be some kind of Dickensian lawyer's clerk, probably started driving before they had tests at all. What's he wearing a hat, in his car, for? And what silly sticking-out ears he has. That's right, you bumbling old fool, slow down as we come to the next lights and we'll miss the green.

See, how he sits motionless when they change to amber. Only when they are green does he wake from his senile doze, you can see his shoulders heaving as he laboriously releases his handbrake (he puts it on at every stop, as though he were on a steep moorland road instead of in suburban traffic) and then he starts wrestling with the gears. Ah come on, you silly old zombie.

Here we are at some more lights. I'm still behind him in the outside lane, but this time there ought to be room for two of us. I make a practice of always checking in my

109

mirror, I can see there's nothing close behind, it'll be perfectly safe for me to move up inside him so we're level at the inevitable red light, then I'll get away while he's still fumbling with his handbrake.

It's no good blowing your horn like that, Dad. You're in a city now, they don't have a man with a red flag walking in front of the horseless carriages any more. There's plenty of room for two cars here. If people would use the space and make two lanes instead of one we'd all get through in half the time, wouldn't we? Some of us have work to do, we're not all on the way to an over-sixties bingo session. . .

Gosh, I just caught a glimpse of him. He could be younger than me. Some people are obviously just *born* old. Naturally, I leave him when the lights change. But of course now I'm on the inside lane again; and wouldn't you know, here I am behind a bus. Can't move out to pass it till old ditherboots dodders past, I can see him nearly alongside me.

Ah come on, you craven, indecisive loon, get on with it. Can't you see I'm waving you on?

At last he does pass me, and I move out, so that I'm behind him again. His offside indicator is *still* flashing. Perhaps he'll notice it when we get past this next lot of lights. They're the last ones before a nice dual-carriageway stretch, and for once they're in our favour. At last I'll be able to get moving.

But what is this? He's stopped dead in front of me, his indicator still flashing. Would you believe it, he wants to turn off! Now we've got to wait for all the oncoming traffic. Hundreds, thousands of us speeding along this important main road and I have to get behind the one man who wants to turn off it into some obscure suburb. All the buses and other traffic I have skilfully (but always courteously) passed for the last two miles are roaring up past us on the inside lane while I wait helplessly behind this bumbling idiot . . .

When all three of us happen to stop at the same garage for petrol, the Man in Front never just has a simple four

110

gallons, like me. He has a whole tankful, and he never pays cash, he has some credit card which involves a lot of fussing with bits of paper and signatures. Then just when I think he's going to move off I see, with a sinking heart, that he's asking a mechanic to look inside the bonnet. At the very least that means he's going to have some oil. Go on, Charlie, get the battery topped up and refill the windscreen-washer thing while you're at it. There's no hurry, I've got all the time in the world.

Ah, he's going to be there all day, I'll back out and move over to this other pump. But before I get a chance to do so the Man Behind zooms up to it, switches off after a great showing-off belching roar, and is instantly served.

Well, at least he is served quickly. So am I after him. I am therefore the next one out, and I observe that the other fellow has at last finished his fussy, involved transactions and is almost moving out. So now the Man In Front has become the Man Behind, and *vice versa*.

Now, this is the thing that worries me. In no time the fellow in front is driving like a timorous spinster, and the one behind gets absurdly impatient when I won't pass on a blind bend or do something equally dangerous. I simply don't know what comes over them. Surely it can't be anything to do with the way I drive. As I told you, I'm a perfectly ordinary, normal driver.

POLICE TALK

I wish I knew how to talk to policemen. They know how to talk to me. They have been taught how to do it in the police college. Their speech is calm, deliberate, like the slow walk back from their white car from which they have stopped me by pulling down a little roller-blind with ominous words: POLICE. STOP.

I daresay they are taught the walk too. I can imagine the sergeant instructor, sitting in a mock-up model car; the eager recruit walks back briskly from the mock-up police car, snapping his notebook open.

111

'No, *no,* Simpson! You look as if you're coming to ask me if the 15th would be all right for cocktails. Do try and remember, you're the policeman. I'm the motorist. At this stage I may not be sure if I've done anything wrong, or if I have, what it is. Let me *worry.* Put that silly notebook away. You get out from your driving side, first, but keep your gloves on. Just stand there for a moment. Wait till Hargreaves has got out on the other side. That's right, Hargreaves, the large clipboard, with some forms on it. Not just a notebook; this is going to take *time.* Now, come on, both of you. But slowly, *slowly.* The longer you take, the sillier things I'm· likely to think of saying, especially when they're read out in court . . .'

It is all very well for policemen. They have these nice dry garages. They have police mechanics who check their cars regularly. Their tyres are automatically replaced (from *my* rates), I daresay after every 5,000 miles.

They have these gloves, heated rear window, clock, and of course radio, with which they could call up other police cars, probably even helicopters, and tanks if it were necessary, if I really did have in the boot some ingots of stolen uranium, or a crate of Certain Substances, or £500,000 in notes from the Great Train Robbery, and tried to make a dash for it.

Of course nine times out of ten I *do* know what they have stopped me for. That confounded footling little plastic licence-holder has come unstuck again.

In the old days, when policemen were still 'bobbies', and had trouser-clips and helmets and, very often, walrus moustaches, licence-holders were solidly fixed to the windscreen. There was this slightly conical metal backing, held in by a spring ring. All you had to do when replacing the licence was to compress this ring, out would come the backing, in would go the new licence. Then backing, then spring, and bob was your uncle.

Now he isn't your uncle at all, and it is no use trying to explain to him that all you seem to be able to buy anywhere is this fool plastic disc, which is supposed to adhere magically to the windscreen if you simply 'take care to exclude air bubbles'. Others may; mine does not.

There are two of him, not in the least like uncles. This Simpson, with a little ginger moustache, and Hargreaves, with dark sideburns, and his intimidating clipboard. They don't have helmets, they have flat caps with a kind of draught-board pattern going round. They are *officers* . . . I think.

People in stories and cartoons are always addressing them as 'Officer'. (Old joke: 'We're investigating a case of sheep-worrying, sir. Have you anything to report?' 'No, thank you, officer, they never worry me.') But I have never actually heard anyone say 'Officer', or even 'Constable.'

They know very well that I do not quite know whether they are officers or not. They know very well what is passing through my mind as they do this interminable spacemen-on-the-moon walk towards my lowered window—especially if, just for once, it is not the licence, it is all in order, stuck up there with eight pieces of Sellotape in a star pattern.

Can it be that offside rear tyre (there seemed to be quite a lot of tread left the last time I looked, but when was that)? Are the indicators doing that fool trick of theirs again, coming on at both sides simultaneously, as if indicating that the car is about to split down the middle?

Has the number-plate fallen off? Surely I wasn't swerving? Surely two Guinnesses wouldn't turn the Breathalyzer green? What the hell *is* a milligram? Gosh, suppose there's a dead dog on the rear bumper? Or maybe it is still an offence if the licence is only held on by eight pieces of Sellotape . . .

At last they speak. 'Good afternoon, *sir.*' There is that in their voices whether it is in Cornwall, Lancashire, or Suffolk, which suggests that really it is I who should be calling them, Sir.

They peer into the car, taking in with one practised sweep the holey carpets, the spindle (or whatever it is) from which the rear offside window handle has come off, the sweet papers (and disgusting half-eaten sweets themselves).

'Good afternoon, sir. Did you realise that your licence is a year out of date?'

By now I should know better than to rattle on about unreliable plastic holders, how last year's licence *had* been lying around in the car for—well, for nearly a year, ha ha, how the children seem to make everything in the car sticky *except* the licence holder. (That's another thing the police don't have to cope with, children in their cars. Give mine half an hour's ride in that immaculate white job of theirs, then we'd see a difference. Their roller blind would be jammed, their radio knobs would be all sticky, their blue flashing light wouldn't flash—and I wouldn't mind betting *their* licence would have fallen off too.)

Never mind all that. It is an offence. Just shut up, just answer yes or no, or else in three weeks' time, just when you are beginning to think that they have decided that anyone with such a complicated excuse is coping so successfully with a complicated but deserving life that no further action should be taken, this summons on green paper will come.

Well, it will come anyway, but at least it will not have typed on it, to be read out later while court clerks snicker behind their hands and the local reporter suddenly picks up his pencil, some such rigmarole as *when questioned, the accused said, 'I thought the one with the jam on it was last year's.'*

Usually, in fact, the words as written down manage to look not only faintly half-witted but vaguely criminal as well. Once I was bowling up the Great North Road, taking the family to Westmorland in *November,* for half-term (what could be more sober, virtuous, law-abiding than that?). The licence was securely up for once, I had checked the indicators; on my car when it is laden with family, there is a toe-in effect on the rear wheels (or is it toe-out?), the tread had looked a bit thin on the inside, but you could see it quite plain on the outside. It was one of those glorious, sunshiny November days. At peace with the world. Good Citizen Jennings.

114

'Why are people so frightened of police cars?' I said to my wife. 'Look at them all, crawling sedately behind it at 40. We're not in the limit, let's get on with it.' I drew out and passed the cowardly procession. I passed the police car leading it. Nothing on *my* conscience. One of my children actually waved to them.

They stuck to our tail for two miles before pulling in front and doing this bit with the roller blind. POLICE. STOP.

It was in one of those empty-looking regions half-way up eastern England, where there is no industry, a lot of mechanised farming, nothing much for the people to do. Half of them join the police and lurk about, trying to catch motorists from more prosperous and hard-working regions, and get fines from them.

Out got Simpson and Hargreaves, or Parfitt and Grugsby, or Snodgrass and White, or whoever they were. Very slowly.

'Good morning, sir,' said Wiggins, with the clipboard. Bradley had some ade of stainless steel, with which he probed the offside rear tyre. 'You seem to have a bald tyre.'

'That's putting it baldly,' I gabbled. 'I suppose I was vaguely worried about that tyre, but not very much. I mean, I simply wasn't thinking of it as *illegally* bald, yet. One has these sort of Lists of Things To Be Done Next, in any family, you know, ha ha. Dental appointment. Kitchen window. Piano tuner. Is the house insured for enough? That tyre was about fifth on the list. I mean, I wasn't *un*-aware of it . . .'

My wife was kicking me and muttering a word that sounded like 'Hist!' But I could not stop. Bradley stared silently at me. 'Could I see your licence, sir?'

'It's stuck up there. With the Sellotape.'

'No sir. Your *driving* licence.'

Well, sucks to him. That was all in order too. He was carefully writing my name and address on the clipboard when he was rejoined by Wiggins, who said 'They're *both* bald.'

115

When the summons came it said *when questioned, the accused replied: 'Oh is the other one bald too?'* As if I'd known all along that one of them was illegal at least, you see.

Just shut up. Just say yes or no. I wish I could.

The only thing that consoles me is hearing about people who say even sillier-sounding things than I do. I read in my local paper of a lad who had recently passed his driving test and was driving an office car out of town. He was in a long residential road, lined with parked cars on both sides, with just room for the two single lines of traffic. He saw a car approaching from the opposite direction. In his anxiety not to hit it, he moved a fraction too close to a parked car on his nearside. His only damage was a bit of red paint on his door handle, but he made a terrible gash along this almost new car (it turned out to cost £80 to repair).

Its owner rushed out of his house, and there was a fairly sharp confrontation. But in the end, having exchanged insurance details and the rest of it, they parted as politely as one can under such circumstances.

This was on a Friday evening. On the following Monday evening the same lad was driving the same car up the same road. He saw the man whose car he had hit, cutting his front hedge. There was no sign of the car (it was already in for repair). To show there was no ill feeling, the man waved.

The lad waved back. Unfortunately this distracted him just enough for him to swerve slightly and, this time, hit an approaching car a not exactly glancing blow. There was a tremendous *katOING* in fact. The usual crowd appeared from nowhere, including of course Friday's victim. And, in a few minutes, the police.

'Well, sir, how did you come to hit this vehicle?' said Hargreaves (or it may have been Simpson).

The lad gave what seems to me an immortal reply, which was later read out in court. 'Well,' he said, 'I was waving at the man I hit on Friday.'

Laughter in court, it said. What I'd like to know is whether Simpson (or Hargreaves) laughed.

Unless you are actually touring or on a long business trip there is rather an element of so-what about those heraldic signs that people put on their cars, saying *Essex,* or *Warwickshire.*

If you're only popping down to the butcher's *in* Essex, or Warwickshire, the information is redundant. If you are in Yorkshire, all the driver behind will learn is what the coat of arms for Warwickshire (or Essex) is. It would be nice to think that if a Somerset driver, finding himself in Northumberland behind another Somerset driver, described as such by one of these plates, were to flash his headlights excitedly, the other fellow would stop, great firkins of cider would be got out from the boot and they would start telling each other terrific dialect stories under Hadrian's Wall—but I'm sure this never happens. I am sure they never even wave at each other.

The Americans, as usual, have this better organised. On an Oklahoma number plate it says OKLAHOMA IS OK, Louisiana says SPORTSMAN'S PARADISE, Arizona is GRAND CANYON STATE. Minnesota has 10,000 LAKES, North Dakota is PEACE GARDEN STATE (although I could swear I have read about silos containing Minuteman H-bomb missiles there), Montana is BIG SKY COUNTRY, New Mexico is LAND OF ENCHANT-MENT, Maine is VACATIONLAND.

Some are historical or hortatory. Delaware drivers tell you proudly that they are THE FIRST STATE, Alaska is NORTH TO THE FUTURE.

It is a bit of a come-down to Idaho, which simply says FAMOUS POTATOES. Well, it wouldn't make a person say 'let's go to Idaho and get some of those famous potatoes', but it might, just, subliminally persuade a New York housewife to insist on Idaho varieties when shopping. All of them say *something* about the region.

With all our regional diversities it is temping to wonder what could be done here. For example:

Surrey	10,000 tennis clubs
	Land of lawn-mowers
	Eternal Guildford
Hampshire	Hearth of cricket
	Retirement Paradise
Leicestershire	Region of Ratepayers
	Visit Kirby Muxloe
Isle of Wight	You can't go wong
	Queen Victoria was amused
Wiltshire	Stonehenge and bacon
Essex	Visit Dagenham
	Where creek meets creek
Sussex	Good yeomen stockbrokers
	Stockbrokers' paradise
Oxfordshire	Land of Carfaxtories
	Birthplace of traffic
Gloucestershire	Air and craft
	Thanks, noble Gloucester
	Cheltenham Ladies 19, Roedean O.
Norfolk	Norwich for capital
	Potatoes and jackets

That is probably how most counties would go; a touch of the atmosphere with, not surprisingly in England, local historical and cultural allusions. However there are other counties which somehow suggest an English equivalent to those Idaho Famous Potatoes, some direct reference to local trades or products:

Staffordshire	Tops in pots
	Black but beautiful
	Leadless glaze country
Somerset	Zider Zee
	Quaffin' Quantocks
	Stay with apples
	Have a good Cheddar Gorge
Worcestershire	What a sauce!
Warwickshire	World bardware centre

Other counties would doubtless use their number-plates

to make a definite, clear-cut statement about their appeal to tourists:

Breconshire   *Huilthy Bealth Wells*
Cornwall   *Land's beginning*
                  England's best point
                  Celts without kilts

As a matter of fact, there is something about the touristic counties which makes the effort of compression into a few syllables—like the discipline of composing a Japanese *haiku*—more difficult; there would be a strong inclination to lengthen the message. With either very small lettering, or a very long number plate, Cornwall could manage something like 'Why buy Devonshire cream when ours is even clottier?'

And Westmorland, instead of something fairly obvious like

> *Dampness is all*
> *Land of umbrellas*

might very easily be tempted into

> *If you must come off the M6 then at least buy something, if it's only a postcard*

But this would be a dangerous precedent. It would open the floodgate for all sorts of political and propaganda messages. Cambridgeshire, for instance, might be tempted to:

> *No connection with East Anglia University*

All the same it would be too much to expect *Welsh* number plates to be as calm as English ones in these days of nationalism; and the limitation of words would be no obstacle, for a nation of poets, to a whole range of patriotism, from that of:

Glamorgan   *Glamourgan*
                 Triple Crown Land

> *For Pally Valleys*
> *See Cardiff and Dai*

to the fiercer stuff of, say:

Caernarvonshire *Peace! Bomb Westminster!*
No pyplyn to Byrmyanghym
Go Hwn Ynglysmyn
Rhynnyng-yn, Plys Pas
Myndd Ywr Owain Bysnys

But there's no doubt that the *best* ones would be those that most successfully managed to compress the essence of their region into some short, simple, memorable phrase in this unique style, somewhere between an advertising slogan and a public signpost:

Derbyshire *Visit an old lead mine*
Best-dressed wells
Famous Fluorspar
Top-whole pot-holing
Lincolnshire *Famous Potatoes*
Potatoes and Poachers
Cathedral and Cabbages

If such phrases also managed to express old traditions and attitudes as well, to contain some sort of mythic or folklore point, so much the better; the whole thing would give Yorkshire and Lancashire, for instance, another field besides cricket in which to perpetuate the Wars of the Roses:

Lancashire *Bright Angelic Mills*
We Get Weaving
Hanker for Lancashire
Land of 10,000 Town Halls
Yorkshire *Land of 10,000 Town Halls*
Land of the Pudding
Leeds in all fields
Is there anywhere else?

Whatever it was, it would be more interesting than those boring coats-of-arms.

Brackett Bros here
I hear you have hundreds of Honda and kindred car spares.

Certainly. Stacked by statistics, catalogue-classed by computer. Check what you want on our check-list.

I reckon my secondhand Honda 800 has sickened and slackened. I wonder—

—a Honda 800? A secondhand Honda 800? They're rare, are those spares. The demand they are under—

None the less, buying it wasn't a blunder, by thunder! No one could find a man fonder than me of his secondhand Honda 800. Convertible-covered, or coupé, Honda 800's respond at the touch (so quick, and to sixty in seconds). But now it has sickened and slackened; a clatter and clank in the clutch when I touch it. But I cannot abandon my Honda. The place where I took it said, 'Look, it's a Honda with specialist spares, we can't mend a Honda, *we* recommend, in effect, you make contact with Brackett and get them to check it.'

A secondhand Honda 800! They're rare, are the spares. They ceased to produce them, the Honda 800 was axed in the Sixties—some date; '68 at the latest. Their spares are the rarest. The greatest good luck if in stock. You're lacking a bracket or sprocket? We'll check it, of course; but even a lock or a jack, it'll cost you a packet, so check if your pocket can stick it. Prices have rocketed, even at Brackett.

Just my luck! Not a mere lug or a lock do I lack. It is larger. I charged the garage where I took it to check it, they said all this clatter and clank in the clutch, the fiddle and fidget to fix it in gear is through wear in the bearing, they're fearing the clutch thrust bearing is wearing.

A clutch thrust bearing! Oh dear, it is rare, is a bearing like that, I don't think we stock it at Brackett. The makers don't make it, you see.

Could you search for it? Search, I beseech you. A *thrush cluts,* or soon all my gears, with no *thruts clush* to push in and mesh them, will smash in the box. If you do have a *crush thluts* in stock (for a Honda 800) I want it so much that you needn't despatch it, I'll come in and fetch it myself.

A clutch thrust plate for a Honda 800, that right?

A *clush thrutch*—it sticks in the throat—a *clutch thrust*, that's right. Not the clutch, but the *plust thrate* that *cushes* the *plutch*.

The thrust plate, ah yes. Ah no, we've not got it at Brackett.

I cannot just sit here, despondent, my Honda redundant. It's wanted, my Honda, depended on. It's not just a Honda with windows that open, you know, a sedately sedan-like saloon all sedentary-solemn and modern in mode. It's a Honda *convertible,* secondhand; hooded, or open and grand if a man demand wind as he rides and is fanned in a Honda, he's sunned in abundance and tanned in one Sunday (or Monday if fine) day. I can't understand how they came to abandon it.

Honda, like all men do, have to plan for demand, and demand for convertibles tended to dwindle and so it was axed in the Sixties. Too out of date is an eight-year-old Honda. If it was later and straighter, we'd cater, we'd quote you complete. But now obsolete.

Obsolete! Absolute balderdash! My wonderful Honda, a hundred more thousands of miles in its Nipponese nippiness: nickel (I know not, but anyway alloy) and needles of nylon for bearings, purring or roaring, with four carburettors, what better or neater or feater (or more to the litre)? It flows as it goes like a bomb, with a hum and a thrum; and so open and free with the rush through fresh air! Not rich like a Rolls, or medium-Mini-minute, or solemn saloon with a comfort of carpets and chrome, but a wonder, a Honda 800 open to thunder and sun. Nothing is wrong with its watchwork witchery, save when I touch on the clutch. *Jush* for a *crutch plate* or *thutch crust,* O curse, must I bend, and abandon my Honda? Come, Brackett, attack it, go search in your stock, it is there I am sure.

Sorry. Don't stock it at Brackett.

Are we stuck, must we chuck it? My Honda now ended,
mechanical miracle merely remembered, a tangle of tin on
a tip or sorry on scrapheap? Just for a *clush,* for a *thrutch,
jush* for one *plutch thrate* bearing?

*Well, we could ring, diversified dealers like Doggetts of
Deptford, Peters of Peckham, Dartford and Deane of
Dover, Parker and Coggett of Poole, if you like, we can
try, might be lucky: or Leckie of Hendon, or Harry and
Larry of Brum . . .*

Try them all, I will pay for the calls. I cannot abandon
my Honda to fate, I will clutch at a straw, I will pester and
question and thrust and withdraw. I'll seek early and late,
and be damned to the date and the wait, I will not
renounce (though I cannot pronounce it) my *crush thutch
plate cluth bust crate bluck blackett* . . . hello, hello, is
that *Blacketts,* hello, hello, HELLO . . .

DEPARTURE LOUNGE

*(On trying to buy a perfectly ordinary notebook in the last-minute
shop near the flight indicator board.)*

....

Imprisoned in glass, every class of passenger waiting
Watching the fidgety flip-flap flight-board indicating;
Duty-free bottles all clinking; blue rinse ladies from
    Milwaukee,
Purposeful, powerful, Paris-or-Persia-bound men on
    Business (capital B),
Their slick-black tray-slot chromium-covered
    document-cases holding
Documents (doubtless . . . or possibly *Playboy,* full-front
    nudes unfolding);
Japanese juveniles solemn-eyed, anorak'd,
    Nipponese-nappied and still;
Noisier-nationaled nippers who whimper and whine and
    whose shriekings are shrill;
A luggageless limbo for Everyman's restless to-ings and
    fro-ings

Before the relief of release to the boarding of Boeings;
Transient travellers, humans all hemmed in a vacuum and
  void,
Hand-baggage only, trapped in a time endured, not
  enjoyed . . .
  Surely, since we need their dough
  There'll be some effort at Heath Row
  To tempt, with merchandise well planned,
  Their last few minutes in our land,
  Some things that Britain still makes well,
  Unknown where all these people dwell;
  Not *big* stuff, like a great Rolls-Royce,
  Just suitable last-minute choice:
  Our sweets and foods they'll surely stock—
  Tart, crumbly Edinburgh Rock,
  Kendal Mint Cake; cheeses, too,
  They'd love a Stilton in Peru
  And homebound Arabs could not fail
  To wow Kuwait with Wensleydale;
  In this short metre no skill can
  Make Farrah's Harrogate Toffee scan,
  But folks would say, in Bonn or Trier
  'You can't get toffee like that *here!*'
  Just think of breakfasts in Belgrade
  With Cooper's Oxford Marmalade
  Smoked trout, or bloaters, would stay fresh
  At least as far as Bangladesh,
  Australian wives would surely hug
  Their husbands, if a Wedgwood mug
  (Or Spode, or Minton) he brought back
  With chaste designs in blue or black,
  Brazilians to their sons would say
  'A little gift for you, Pepe' . . .
  'Papa! A Sheffield pocket knife!
  I'll cherish it through all my life!'
  This is the stuff they ought to sell,
  But in that gift-shop . . . do they hell!
With a captive market, a tumult of tourists, there's only a
  jumblejorum

Of trivial tat, as if *trying* with trumpery tawdry to bore
     'em,
Knock-me-down knick-knacks, fantastic and drastic in
     taste,
Churchills in china, policemen in polythene, globular
     fur-covered gonks with no waist,
Sub-luxurious carvings, holders and folders and requisites
     moulded,
Scissors and nailsets and combs, but in luxury leather
     enfolded,
Costly contrivances not of a national provenance, not
     really British
Though carrier bags and trumpery mugs have the Union
     Jack painted (all skittish),
Dull international flotsam and jetset jazz, figurines as ugly
     as sin,
Unwantable wares making airfarers wonder what country
     they're in;
A few books—pornographic, or lewdly adorned if they're
     Hardy or Dickens
With Jezebel jackets that nudge how a sexy plot
     thickens...

          Alas, when all is said and done
          No departure lounge is fun
          And that is why this verse is written.
          Let us pioneer in Britain,
          Fill this claustrophobic space
          With all the glories of our race;
          Let *ideas,* like aircraft soaring,
          Make the shop less bloody boring.

ALONE BUT NOT POSH

To hear some people talk you would think there were only
two kinds of air traveller: Alone/Posh and Group/Vul-
gar—hereinafter referred to, as they say in contracts, as
AP and GV.

125

The AP traveller is a suave, mysterious man smelling of after-shave lotion, wearing pigskin gloves and equipped with dark matching luggage and a very expensive, light, casual waterproof. Now and again he consults an electronic watch guaranteed to lose no more than 3 seconds every 1,000 years.

He may be really Alone, this lean figure in the well-cut suit, in which case he is quite likely to be some kind of very high-class secret diplomat or spy, perfectly competent to disable five thugs in striped jerseys who set on him in some ill-lit alley. Or he may have a lady AP with him, a haughty dolly with those sucked-in cheeks, smelling of expensive after-chiffon scarves and money. She may or may not be his wife. They have come from some very grand house built of pale stone in Gloucestershire in 1711, and are on their way to a spot of boar-hunting with their friend M. le Comte. AP travellers are met at the arrival gate by chauffeurs with *shiny leggings*.

GV travellers (in the plural, naturally) on the other hand, are a noisy lot. They all live in the same street in some place with a name like Bog Mills, Cogheap, Bleakbury, Clangbotham or Thrike Moor. They are all 50 and drink beer incessantly. The men wear brown or blue suits with open-necked tennis shirts, the women have fat knees and print dresses and keep shrieking with laughter.

They are on a package tour, of course—or, even worse, a charter flight. And somehow it is suggested that there is something ignoble, something lowering to the human personality in GV flying.

Well, I dunno. I've done a lot of both kinds. Not of course that *I've* got a 1711 house in Gloucestershire. Far from it. I've got six children. I've got a garden full of nettles and ground elder; our first and probably last washing-up machine has got so that if you forget to turn off the main tap when it has finished roaring and hissing and cementing bits of rice on to the tumblers it floods the kitchen floor two inches deep, and we can't afford another one just now because the garage is going to fall down any minute and the wallpaper is a disgrace in the hall and there

126

is that bit where the carpet is worn and we seem to buy three duffel coats a month and and and . . . well, I may sometimes fly Alone but when I do it's certainly not Posh.

As a matter of fact the boot is on the other foot or, to coin a metaphor it is time we had in the jet age, the wing is on the other shoulder. It isn't only that in GV flying one has the luxury of being with friends or family. It's this very thing of being a human parcel, of not having to think, of having things done for you, despised by AP travellers as sheep-like and sub-human, that in itself constitutes a blissful luxury for me.

Maybe it's something to do with having six children (which no AP traveller would be seen dead with. AP travellers have never even been children themselves; they are born, fully equipped with all that pigskin, etc., aged 30). With six children, you spend a lot of your time just *counting*. And trying to remember if the hair brush is in the Big Case. And opening little cardboard pyramids of cream without squirting it all over the place. And saying, well you can't *all* sit by the window. And re-counting. I've always wanted to persuade some plastics firm to make a modern lightweight version of the old convict's ball and chain, but instead of the ball there would be this light plastic suction pad with which you could clamp say three of them to the wall so they didn't get lost while you went to find the other three, in the duty-free shop or staring at the carousel unloading the luggage of an incoming flight from Reykjavik). And, oh God, has anybody seen the little black case with the zip, it's got all the money and the passports in it, and and and . . .

Actually you can't manage much flying at all, even GV, with six children. But even without them, there are occasions when I quite envy the GV parties, with someone to do all the deciding for them. It's not that I can't decide for myself (it's no good the real AP man sneering quietly to himself as he reads this; he's got a secretary who does the real work and finds out what time the dark blue Merc has to be sent to his door. Your real AP man is cocooned from harsh reality by this host of menials). When I fly Alone

I'm the one who does all the telephoning and humping bags from Gloucester Road tube station to the Air Terminal up a lot of spiral concrete staircases, because the AP travellers' secretaries have grabbed all the taxis in London.

And precisely because of this I am much more aware than they are of how much there is to be taken off one's shoulders by travelling GV. The whole flying business is such a world-wide, interlocked, delicately adjusted affair—not only the aircraft themselves, but all those radio and Telex messages, controllers on the ground handing over flights to each other, little flags on maps, radar blips, weather reports, showrooms, head offices, floor polish, computers, mysterious red-and-white striped trailers on airfield perimeters, the whole complicated set-up. One false move and you're in Bombay, or you're booked for the 15th of *next* month, or you've lost your little black case with the zip—or, most likely, your flight.

Once I was flying to Manchester. From London. Simple domestic flight, easy as getting on a bus. I was going to take part in the radio programme *A Word in Edgeways*. I got to the Terminal at the time it said. I got on the right coach. On it I met a journalist acquaintance. He was going to Manchester too (or it may have been Bombay, or he had just come back from Bombay. Anyway, he kept on about not having had any breakfast).

At the airport he said he would set up a couple of coffees for us while I went to find the insurance machine (I'm their best customer. I love flying, in fact I've been up in a hot air balloon too, for the Telegraph Magazine; but I've got these six children. One day some man is going to go to one of these machines and the moment he presses the knob £9,999 in coins all put in by me over the years, will gush out in a tremendous jackpot).

I was, at most, five minutes doing this. When I got back to the coffee place there was no sign of my friend (my friend?). It was 10.40, and take-off was 11.20. Well, I thought, maybe he's gone to the restaurant or somewhere to get a proper breakfast (he was Scots, after all; they have to start the day with all this porridge and oatie cakes and stuff). I ordered two coffees, in case he turned up, and waited for the flight to be announced.

I didn't read the paper, or do the crossword, or let my attention wander. We know a thing or two, we ANP (Alone but Not Posh) travellers. I kept my mind on the business in hand, I listened carefully to all the announcements. They kept on and on saying, with increasing desperation, 'Will Mr Walsh, passenger on Aer Lingus Flight A47 to Cork, *please* report to Gate 6.'

Gosh, I thought, they're going to be pretty sharp with that Walsh when he does turn up.

10.45, 10.50, 10.55. They would be calling the Manchester flight any minute now; not one of your fussy, over-organised, called-miles-too-early international flights. Just popping up to Manchester. Chaps do it every day. 11.00, 11.05.

I strolled over to the desk and asked the girl if they would be calling the Manchester flight soon.

'It was called at 10.35, as soon as the coach came,' she said. 'Gate 7, but it's closed now, I should think.' I rushed to Gate 7. It was in the days when you went down a lot of zig-zag ramps, and I went down one too many. I found myself running on ground level with the stair closing down on me, like the bit under the stairs at home. I rushed back up to where the door was. And there was the aircraft on the apron, its engines already started. They wouldn't let me through.

One thing I found out that day. If you sit all by yourself in a BBC studio in London, connected by what they quaintly call 'a land-line' to a radio discussion in Manchester, totally unable to intimate that you want to break into the conversation except by coughing, it is better to do it under an assumed name (like Walsh, maybe).

In GV travel you are shielded from this kind of thing. Someone else is responsible. Most of my GV travel has been with press parties, where such worries as one has are concerned either with getting a different story from everyone else when you are all going to the same place, or with not drinking so much on the aircraft that one can't last out the subsequent cocktail party, followed by tremendous formal dinner with flowery 'our two-countries-linked-by-tourist-friendship' toasts. Or it has been with about 180 other members of the New Philharmonia Chorus.

Three, four, five times a year we get into some aircraft (sometimes jet, sometimes with eight propellers and wicker chairs and wire struts) and go to Italy, or Spain, or France. Audiences in splendid marble halls and theatres throw down carnations at the front rows of sopranos and give us terrific civic receptions. Our tickets are dished out to us, we are taken everywhere in buses, we occupy entire hotels, and we don't have to *think* about anything except singing and enjoying ourselves. And none of us would change places with the poshest AP passenger in the world.

PART THREE

AT HOME AND ABROAD

....

It's funny how it has got about that the great thing to do if you have a family of any size is to go camping. Two or three years ago I bought a minibus because after bringing one wife and six children in a Ford Consul convertible from Lahinch (County Clare, Eire) to East Bergholt (Suffolk, England)—that is, just about the longest west-east journey it is possible to make in these islands—I practically had to put them in water to get them back to their proper, uncompressed size, like those Japanese paper flowers.

I didn't buy it to go camping in. I bought it because the children could sit round a table reading or get up and walk about as though they were in a tiny public library—and a public library where you can make cups of tea, what's more, since it has a little stove with two gas rings. And all this while whizzing up the motorway at 60. I bought it for the space. Sometimes I forget where the engine is, it seems impossible to believe that one of those cupboards (most of them *are* cupboards, stacked with suitcases, water containers, saucepans, kitchen stuff that makes a subdued merry tinkling and jingling when I brake suddenly) contains a neat but powerful engine which propels this—this *room* along.

But we don't camp in it. Picnics, yes, including winter ones, and it is very nice to come back from the howling wind on some deserted beach, get into this thing and steam up the windows doing chops or toast or cocoa. But the first thing anybody says, seeing it for the first time, is, 'Ah, I suppose you find it very useful for camping.'

What, eight of us? It's hard enough cooking for that lot with an Aga, let alone two gas rings in a place where you can't stand up straight. It was hard enough camping in it, just myself alone, when I was going round the country getting material for a book on rural England.

It's true the minibus was my office, my kitchen and my bedroom—but never all at once. Once you actually make the double bed you've lost your table and any space to stand, even doubled up (moreover I hate making a bed that I am actually kneeling on at the time). I seemed to be forever folding, groping, lifting, washing, stretching, climbing over partitions, moving things off flat cupboard lids, creeping about like the Hunchback of Notre Dame, especially when it was raining, as it usually was, and I couldn't go outside to fold those great big bodgy blankets.

It's true, also, that in the brochure which the garage where I bought this thing kindly gave me (since it wasn't new; nobody has six children *and* a new minibus) there was a picture of a smiling, thirtyish couple having tea under a striped awning, sitting in smart aluminium chairs at a smart aluminium table, on a sunny day somewhere in the Black Forest, with their two smiling children. But that, to me, is the absolute upper limit both in age of parents and size of family for camping.

And even then you'd have to be pretty keen on it. You'd have to buy either the special tent you can get with this minibus, which kind of zips on to the side of it, or an ordinary tent, one with four sides to it (if you were us you'd have to get a marquee). And you couldn't stop there. You'd have to get all those awful little chairs and stools and tables and lots of gadgety things with spindly legs, made of some very light metal, and with a lot of straps and nylon cords and toggles; a sort of thin, ghostlike reflection of the real, solid furniture of ordinary domestic life, but all reduced to extreme functionalism, and all very light.

When I think what our children do to quite heavy things the idea of letting them loose on this gossamer stuff is laughable. Short-sighted visitors peering into our playroom say, 'Oh, I didn't know you had a harp.' It isn't a harp, it's the gold-painted, ultimately irreducible iron framework of an old upright piano which we once bought and put in there in the mistaken hope that they would practise on their 'own' piano. (What a hope, they won't even practise on the boudoir grand. I've seen them actually jumping up and down on the keys of this upright, once enough of those confounded little felt things on the end of fatally breakable thin wooden rods had been broken for it to be accepted that it was beyond repair.)

We have a lot of heavy tin mugs—we'd get them of cast-iron with lead bottoms if we could—and even so they keep knocking them over. Let them loose among all those delicate little frying pans and families of lightweight saucepans and those dinky little stoves with fragile tubes connected to smart bottles of some smart French gas, or rather gaz—why, they'd wreck it (not on purpose, you understand; merely in the course of ordinary living) in five minutes.

Sooner or later the idea of France was bound to come up, because this is really what is at the back of the minds of those who think our minibus is for camping. They see us effortlessly treading that supposed new and simple path to holiday joy, the modernised continental, and especially French, system of proper sites, proper equipment and so on. It is true the French have been able to set about it with more confidence, more belief in the thing as an industry, because of their climate.

They do have these sophisticated blue and orange tents with actual corridors, no doubt leading to lightweight aluminium lavatories infinitely more sophisticated than the ones in their hotels. They have these chains of well-conducted sites, with restaurants and rules of silence at 11 p.m. and the rest of it.

From where I'm sitting there are two objections to this. One is that our children jump about more than French children. I'm quite ready to admit that once French children become what are known as Young People they jump about quite a lot, especially on beaches, where they keep kicking big wet medicine balls into your picnic. But when they are children they are solemn, rather pasty-faced creatures who seem to stay put wherever their parents have propped them up.

The other is, precisely, that the thing is well organised, it is an industry. What's the point of camping if you can't be in the real wild country and make a great fire to keep bears away, or grill trout which you have just caught in the mountain stream that flows past the lonely clearing where your tent is pitched?

If you're going to pitch in a well-lit site just off a *route nationale* where you are surrounded by people fully equipped not only with all this aluminium furniture and gaz but with transistors (and who have, at most, two of those apathetic children) you'd be much better off staying every night at the admirable hotels (and never mind about the lavatories) you find in the smallest town, until you get to wherever you're staying (and if you have six children it won't be in a tent; which is why we don't get to the continent every year).

Camping is for the young; either solitary, or just the opposite, in the formal togetherness of scouting or military service; and it may be just carried over into the honeymoon period, but that would be only for rather special, poetic people, such as those in William Empson's poem *Camping Out*:

> *And now she cleans her teeth into the lake*
> *Gives it (God's grace) for her own bounty's sake*
> *What morning's pale and the crisp mist debars:*
> *Its glass of the divine . . .*

The whole poem is about human existence and love giving meaning to the cold universe, and of course there's no reason why this shouldn't go on for the whole of married life. But that's not to say one must go camping with six children—in a minibus *or* a tent.

Besides, what children, indeed all people, want on a holiday is change, and there's nothing more the same than a tent, once you've put it up. We are fortunate in having the facilities for a kind of dress rehearsal, with all the exciting bits and none of the boring ones, for camping every year.

We've *got* a tent, a proper green English tent with a fly sheet that goes over the top; its two stout buttonholes fit over spikes on the two end poles, if one had little flags flying from them it would indeed look like a small marquee. And the moment we have two warm days

136

together, they take this thing out to the bit of scruffy no-man's-land beyond the garden and put it up.

Each year there are more tears in the groundsheets, more tent pegs are missing, the roof sags more drunkenly because one of the proper poles, taken for some other enterprise during the winter and lost, has to be replaced with a broomstick. But there is a fire, there is much lugging about of camp beds, when we go to say goodnight we can see torch beams flashing in the dim green interior and hear giggling or cries of 'Ow!' and 'Shut up!' and, 'that's *my* pillow', and all the radio stations of Europe, one after another.

All the *nice* part of camping, while we're still in a proper bed ourselves. When cold wind and rain set in the next morning at about 10.30, they will have had one magical morning awakening with the sun shining out of a clear sky on to their temporary home, they will have smelt the dew and make some awful bacony messes in a blackened frying pan, but now they can come right back in and have lunch made on the Aga, as usual, and go back to jumping on the piano and other normal pursuits.

In the ensuing weeks they wander back to the tent for an hour or so, but really the desire has passed for the time being. After a week or so of solid rain it becomes clear that, as usual, if the thing isn't to rot away I shall be the one that has to dismantle it, dry it and fold it up.

And as I fold camp beds, and find beneath them old bits of bread, apple cores, vests, banana skins, comics, socks, sticky sweets, as I try to pull pole sections out of metal (aluminium, no doubt) sleeves in which the damp has caused them to swell and become immovable, as I fold up the guy ropes in neat spirals which come undone and get into tangles when I am folding the still far from dry fly sheet, as the tent pegs, by now a motley collection, fall through the rotted bottom of the tent-peg bag which they had left out in the long grass and took me then minutes to find, I find myself thinking ever more gratefully, thank goodness this isn't a holiday.

To my mind there are two quite separate kinds of swimming, and I don't just mean crawl and breast stroke. I mean Hero and Fun.

It is true that these two sets of terms do overlap a little; probably most Hero swimming is done with the crawl. But mine are much wider than the mere technical definitions of the stroke. They involve the whole life-philosophy and personality of the swimmer. I would like, but do not quite dare, to say that a Hero swimmer is unlikely to be a Fun person.

Hero swimming (and this has nothing to do with the fellow who swam the Hellespont—he was called Leander; the *girl's* name was Hero; very confusing, I've always thought. We've no evidence that she swam at all, but my guess is that if she had she'd have been a Fun swimmer)—as I was saying, Hero swimming is the puroseful, dedicated kind, where people have their heads under the water for nine-tenths of the time.

Fun swimmers hardly ever get their noses wet in calm water. They spend most of their time floating on their backs, gazing dreamily at fleecy, white clouds in a blue sky (if it isn't this kind of day they won't even *be* there), pondering happily on the allness of everything and yet its oneness. Or they do a hopeless surface dive, such that by the time their feet are under, their head has come up again. Or they may call out something witty to those on the beach.

But Hero swimmers probably don't open their eyes, and certainly don't turn on their backs, till they are practically out of sight of *all* land.

You can't tell just by looking at a person which kind of swimmer he is. Quite often an immensely muscular and bronzed Adonis, wearing one of those very professional-looking, many-times-washed faded blue linen loin-cloths, will rush straight down the beach, fall dramatically forward in 18 inches of water and lash out with the most tremendous Hero-type crawl you ever saw—for about six strokes.

Then he simply stands up in the water, meditatively pouring water over his shoulders, or he may even simply come out again, shaking his head vigorously and snorting, and go on to some of that loose-armed trotting that you see athletes doing on the television, between getting off their track suits and getting down to the starting blocks.

On the other hand you may see some thin, inconspicuous fellow, probably an accountant, walk unostentatiously but purposefully into the water, with absolutely no gasping or splashing or demonstration of any kind, and when the water is up to his chest strike out with some Hero stroke until he is a little black dot seen now and again in the waves. After a quarter of an hour you remember him, you find yourself scanning the water quite anxiously. Is that a buoy out there by the headland, or is it him, or is it anything at all, should you perhaps call the coastguard?

On the whole Hero swimmers are solitaries, and it is probably better that way, since when they do get gregarious they spoil things for everyone else. They need a ball of some kind to get gregarious with. There is a great deal of splashing and plunging, ducking each other, snorting and holding their noses, and shouting.

Fun swimmers know in their hearts that man can't beat water. Even when one has learnt to swim they are moments when one realises this afresh. I remember a whole day spent on Lac Léman at Geneva trying to learn to water-ski. If those little Swiss girls, holding on with one hand and waving nonchalantly with the other, could do it, so could I.

I would sit on the end of the jetty holding the towing-bar, the boat would swerve out as slowly as it dared—and the next moment I was being dragged along under ten feet of roaring green water, the whole element contemptuously, murderously, coldly opposing my efforts to stand up. Then I would be forced to let go. The skis would try to drown me by floating up so that my head went back and under.

At last I would manage to kick them off, and there I

139

was, utterly alone. I could see a distant skyline of Geneva, well beyond my Fun swimming range. The boat seemed to have disappeared.

Sailors are the chaps who are really in the business of Man versus Water, and it's a well-known fact that few of *them* can swim, and if they can it's not Hero swimming they do. Sailors realise that if the water is going to get you and you're going to be shipwrecked (which can happen on rocks within view of municipal streetlights as well as in mid-Atlantic) you'll only prolong the agony by a few hours (or, if it's in the Arctic, by a few minutes) if you can swim well.

If, however, you fall into a canal or drive your car over the edge of a dock, a little easy Fun swimming, your head well above water all the time, will be just as much use as all that Hero stuff. Besides, who wants to have his head under all the time if he's swimming in a dock in all that horrible oily mess!

Now that my children are learning to swim (the ones that have made it so far are all Fun swimmers, I'm happy to say), I can see where I went wrong when I was a child trying to learn—or rather where those who tried to teach me went wrong. For all teachers of swimming are, naturally, Hero swimmers, and they mistakenly try to make all their pupils do likewise.

They don't realise that one is *born* either a Hero or a Fun swimmer and there is absolutely nothing they or anyone else can do about it. For years and years, while muscular men in singlets shouted at me from the edge of the water, I would do five frantic strokes of the 'dog paddle' which they all think is an easy, natural prelude to the crawl, and then flounder to my feet in four feet of water. And the sink-or-swim method didn't work either. When I did five frantic strokes and floundered to the bottom in seven feet of water they just had to come in and get me.

Now that I can swim (I once swam 75 lengths, and I only stopped then because I was bored, not tired. It took *hours*; but I could swim the Atlantic in a couple of years) I still can't do the dog paddle. What's so natural about it?

I'm a man, not a dog. And in any case I've looked at dogs swimming, and they don't trail their hind paws behind in a crawl kick, which is what we were supposed to do in this wretched dog paddle. You might just as well expect a dog to do that arm-over-arm stuff with its front paws as ask a human being, like me, to paddle in a way that seems to drag the head under all the time.

What dogs do is sort of walk about in the water; and it looks very like Fun swimming to me. Certainly *they* keep their heads above water all the time.

Yet the boys who were born Hero swimmers took to this absurd, artificial, so-called dog paddle quite naturally. For them it *was* the natural prelude to the crawl, and in no time they were flashing up and down the pool, arms and legs flailing, eyes closed, head buried, pear-shaped mouth gulping in air at every fourth stroke or whatever it is.

I gave it up as a bad job till one wonderful afternoon when I was all of 15 and I thought, I'll just have a go at this despised, womanish breast stroke. I did a width, instantly. Scarcely believing my achievement, I did a length. I let my legs come down, out of my depth for the first time in my life, still idly doing the same stroke. I was treading water. I turned on my back, idly pushing the water down with my hands. I was floating. I saw a long life of happy Fun swimming before me.

But I always resent those Six Lost Years of the dog paddle and failed crawl, of the attempt to make me a Hero swimmer. You can make rules about and actually describe Hero swimming, the way you can describe geometry, I grant that. Although, as I say, Hero swimmers are born not made. There is an element of the formal, the text-book, the *teachable* about their way.

It is we Fun swimmers who are the really instinctive ones. I've been looking at frogs recently. No one will deny that they know a damn sight more about swimming than dogs do. And there's none of this paddling rot about frogs. They do a kind of breast stroke. It's well known that the human embryo passes through a frog-like stage anyway. Fun swimmers have a deep ancestral connection with the womb and the primal sea from which all life developed.

You can't teach Fun swimming. I've found that out with my children. God knows I tried, perhaps as a hangover from all those years with the men in singlets. I tried to teach them because I wanted to get at them young, before *they* had to go through this dog paddle stuff. I would lie across a stool, on dry land, demonstrating the Fun breast stroke, how your ARMS are pulling you forward while your LEGS kick like THIS, *aaagh aagh pant*. (It's even more difficult swimming on a stool; just try it.) But they just sank, as I used to, after four strokes.

I did it in the end by taking them on holiday to a hotel in a warm country with its own swimming pool in a place where I knew there would be mostly Fun swimmers, for it was a lakeside resort (Lugano). Lakes, especially Italian ones, where you can lie face upwards in green water and gaze at romantic villas and cypresses and fountains and gentle bosky hills, attract nice lazy Fun swimmers. Although we appreciate the greater buoyancy of salt water at the seaside we soon get tired of battling with waves and under-tow and Hero polo Players.

By the end of the holiday all those who could walk could swim. My eldest daughter swam an effortless Fun breast stroke, like me. Her younger brother, at the end of the first week, could swim quite well, but only under water. *Very* frog-like, that was. In the second week he found out that he could come up for air and then get on with it down below. With great restraint I didn't tell him anything, and in the last two days he discovered for himself about breathing all the time and keeping the head out of the water.

But it's the smallest of the swimmers I'm most proud of, although in a way it disproves my whole theory. What he does, at the age of six, thrashing up and down the pool in a way that would give me a heart attack after one length, is something I wouldn't have thought possible: a Fun dog paddle.

In the unlikely event of my being commissioned to paint a great fresco of Heaven and Hell I should know just how to do Hell. There would be no flames and pitchforks, just this great windowless room lit by dim naked bulbs. In the stale cigarette smoke, round an enormous table littered with duplicated sheets of incredible boringness, would be slumped the damned, *at a committee meeting that went on for ever.*

Not that this would be an original vision. In *Paradise Lost* Milton represents Pandemonium (literally 'all the devils') as a committee meeting with Satan as chairman, as one devil after another gets up to make a long boring speech about what to do next after the Fall.

But Satan would not be the chairman in my version. One of the damned would preside; and when the meeting had already gone on for thousands of years this chairman, suddenly seeing a hope of moving at last to the next point on the interminable agenda, would say, 'Well, gentlemen, I think there's nothing more to be added to that until the finance subcommittee's report is received . . .'

And then Satan, or some other devil, would get up and say, 'On a point of order, Mr Chairman; there is a little discrepancy in these accounts . . .' And they would all be back to square one.

The trouble is, it isn't heil for lots of people. They actually enjoy being on committees. They like the procedure, the formality, the standard phrases; it is like some elaborate old court dance, only sitting down all the time. They like addressing old Jim, whom they have known for years, as 'Mr Chairman'.

One committee man can tell another by instinct, and I've never quite been able to understand why they are always so keen to get a few obvious non-committee men, such as myself, to join them. In a weak moment I confess to an interest in the thing their committee is concerned with and suddenly there I am, in another dreary room, listening to the Apologies For Absence (gosh, that's a

143

good idea, I think, too late). Maybe they need a few passive members.

At various times I have been astonished to find myself on committees concerned with refugees, a parish dance, a civic ball (How? My wife and I are terrible dancers, we bang our knees together all the time), orchestral concerts, local theatre and old school rugby football. And it is because of these dyed-in-the-wool committee types that all of these meetings have seemed exactly the same, except that as the dread routine becomes familiar each meeting is more boring than the last. Sometimes I make a real effort. I go to the meeting well primed, my head full of constructive ideas for Any Other Business (Item Seven on the Agenda). But after an hour and a quarter we are usually still on Item Two (Accounts and Balance Sheet), and once again I can see that the choice is going to be between Any Other Business and missing my train.

When I have painfully digested the Balance Sheet I turn to the next page where it says Cash at Bank. And there is a totally different set of figures, apparently having no connection whatever with the first page.

While I am staring hopelessly at some such item as 'loan of copies', and wondering why it's on the credit side (dammit, we had to pay for them, didn't we?) somebody says, 'Mr Chairman, could we know why the 60% increase in printing costs (now where did he find *that*?) is set against Contingencies and not Administration?' Or something.

Then, of course, someone else gives his reasons why it should be set against some third heading. They say a camel is a horse designed by a committee, but in my experience that is a pretty good shot at it. I should expect a horse-designing committee to come up with something possessing several different kinds of legs, and also much smaller than the original expectation. A spider would be near the mark.

The fact is that the larger the committee is and the longer its meetings the less it achieves. There is no reason why most decisions could not be arrived at by three people scribbling on the backs of envelopes in a bar. In fact they usually *are* arrived at by three people, but they have to call themselves the Chairman, the Secretary and the Treasurer and nobody thinks their decisions count until they have gone through all this ritual of Minutes and Agenda and Points of Order and the rest of it with anything up to 20 other people.

And it is never in a cheerful place like a bar. It may be in someone's office kindly loaned for the occasion. As I go up the stairs cheerful throngs, released from work, looking forward to an evening of relaxation, the best part of the day, are clattering down them. Or it may be in some dingy school, or even in someone's home, in which case there might be pale milky tea and plain biscuits at half-time.

I once went to a committee meeting and had, for domestic reasons, to leave at eight p.m., when it had already been going for two hours. But I thought I couldn't be missing much. We had got to Item Six (Raising of Subscription. And incidentally who ever heard of a committee lowering a subscription?) I had said my bit, (keep it the same—I always say this, but they always raise it), and thought there was only Item Seven, the last one to deal with. Appointment of Auditors, it was. The merest formality. Surely the most dedicated committee man couldn't do much with the Appointment of Auditors?

But I learnt the next day that the meeting had gone on for another two and a quarter hours. I had forgotten what the Auditors were called, but lets us assume it was the usual trinity of unlikely names, such as Messrs Snarson, Gragsby and Funtpool. Could I have missed some tre-mendous drama of accusation and counter-accusation? I imagined un-imaginable scenes in that dull room.

'You know as well as I do, Mr Chairman, that Snarson is an alcoholic. Gragsby has been convicted of defacing posters, and Funtpool is a Mafia front man, even if he is the Secretary's son-in-law.'

'With respect, Mr Chairman, I do not think the meeting will follow Mr Snocket in wanting to retain the services of Messrs Wabb, Turmeric and Snocket after last year's affair of the Holding Fund.'

'Just step outside and say that again. I'll throw this cold tea in your face . . .'

But no such luck, nothing so interesting as that. Committee people avoid drama at all costs. In fact you could say that a committee meeting is the *opposite* of drama. Do you know what they had been doing all that two and a quarter hours? Still going on about Raising the Subscription, that's what.

What's more, I am sure they enjoyed every minute of it. Sometimes I wonder if they ever stop, if they carry on like this when they're not actually at meetings. I imagine the committee man going home and being asked by his wife if he's had a good day.

'I think I can answer that, Madam Wife. In general it was quite up to the standard of previous days, and I think we may all take encouragement from that. However, I put it to you that it is time we, as a Society, re-examined the transport position. Of course, we all know that this matter has already been well thrashed out at, er, somewhat stormy meetings in the past. But the figures for commuter rail traffic in this area show, as you will have seen from my report, an increase of 23 per cent over last year. This does, I submit, make it difficult for the Hon Wage Earner to get to his place of work in first-class condition and I therefore move that he be empowered to use the Society's vehicle, which after all is a valuable fixed asset.

If his wife is a normal non-committee person she will reply, 'But, George, if you use the car to go to the office I'll be stuck here all day, and it's nearly a mile to the shops.' But if she talks the lingo too, she will begin, 'As House Secretary I must point out that this might create more problems than it would solve . . .' And they will be at it for hours, perhaps referring the whole matter to a Sub-Committee (a marriage guidance bureau) in the end.

Unlikely, perhaps. But there is no doubt that thousands of perfectly normal, articulate, businesslike people turn into stilted ditherers once they are on a committee. Why?

Maybe they think it's more democratic this way?

146

Maybe, they think, only dictators make quick decisions. Mussolini made debates run to time as well as the trains?

If so, let them beware. As they ramble on, raising Points of Order (what does it mean, why not put *Points*?) chasing trivial details like a mad housewife after a single speck of dust, alluring visions of our democratic armchairs and our democratic slippers will form in the minds of the rest of us. Our rumbling democratic stomachs will remind us of the meals, growing cold, prepared by our loving and democratic wives. As they drone on glassy-eyed, self-hypnotised, they will not even notice as one by one we steal away to our democratic homes, perhaps calling in for a much needed democratic drink on the way.

Meanwhile other figures, grimly prepared to wait indefinitely, figures who never find the chairs too hard, will take our places, including eventually even Mr Chairman's, and suddenly a very undemocratic rap of the gavel will halt them in full flight . . .

No, anything but that. We will sit it out.

But keep it short.

COVERED

Every so often I get out an ever bulkier file marked *Insurance*. For a rewarding meditation on the Meaning of Existence it is every bit as useful as what our grandfathers used to call 'spiritual reading'. The other day, visiting a marvellous country house in Ireland, I saw a beautiful little brass-bound teak box, about a cubic foot, which turned out to be a travelling library full of miniature volumes with titles such as: *Witherspoon on Regeneration, Flavel on Providence, Watson on Divine Contentment,* and *Owen on Sin.* Well, in my insurance file today I just found a little booklet by the chaps who insure my house in which it said 'the Company's actuarial valuations are made upon a very stringent basis' (note that 'upon', not just 'on'; I bet Flavel and Witherspoon always said 'upon') . . . profits were calculated by the *British Offices' Ultimate Mortality*

147

Tables' (my italics).

Does not that conjure up a fine mournful picture, as of some classical alabaster tomb of the eighteenth century, with weeping nymphs, faded garlands, pensive figures leaning on urns:

> *Mortality, behold and fear*
> *What a change of flesh is here*

. . . and so on? Yet the curious thing is that within the context of this grand philosophical vision, blinking nothing, one does not feel that the philosophers who know the grand, sombre secrets of the British Officers' Ultimate Mortality Tables turn to our bustling everyday life with a weary sigh. On the contrary, one feels, with Wordsworth (you see what I mean about spiritual reading) that although:

> The clouds that gather round the setting sun
> Do take a sober colouring from an eye
> That hath kept watch o'er man's mortality:
> Another race hath been, and other palms are won.

As we get bulkier ourselves, along with our insurance files, we are surprised to find some palms *have* been won. We may regret the vast premiums we now have to pay if we want to start any more insurance at our time of life, when there's all that mortality about, and sigh at the laughably small amounts you have to pay if you're under thirty (dammit, we were all busy in the army with no time or money to think about civilian luxuries like insurance until we were thirty, so it's all too late now). And yet here I am, with a house, and carpets, and clocks, and beds and things, all of which are insured—indeed have to be, with these chaps, because I don't actually own the house yet, it's on some complicated endowment-policy mortgage.

It is when I look at the correspondence about insuring these things that I am struck by the concern of insurance people with the red-blooded life that precedes mortality. As I see it there are two elements in insurance, just as in roulette or any other game; Predictable and Chance. The

148

former deals with the straightforward regular payment of premiums and the ultimate receipt of a cheque in the evening of one's life: just a glorified form of saving, really. But the other is constantly aware that man has but a short time, he cometh and behold the goeth, etc—but *anything* can happen to him on the way. I used to imagine that Chance—the kind of insurance which at its worst the customer can never experience because he will be dead, he will never know if they pay up on those little cards bought from the machine at the airport, it's like wondering whether the light in the refrigerator really goes out when you shut the door—was in a quite separate part of the insurance office. I used to imagine papers pinned on the staff notice board saying things like, 'while alterations are being made in the Chance canteen arrangements have been made for personnel to take their tea break in the Predictable canteen at 11.15 a.m. and 4 p.m. Please adhere to these times'. The Chance people would be younger, more dashing and imaginative, indeed creative, and many of them would move over to the soberer Predictable some time during their forties.

But from my house insurance documents it is clear that all insurance people know about both sides, indeed, this is their whole glory and mystery. You'd think there couldn't be anything more predictable, prosaic and bourgeois than a house, with all those cushions and beds and saucepans. But even the original policy is full of dramatic stuff about Malicious Persons acting on behalf of or in connection with any political organisation. I see them mumbling behind bushes, suddenly making a concerted rush, trampling all over my herbaceous as they yell their uncouth Maoist slogans. They have been sent out from the city, with instructions to molest Jennings, or at least damage his said dwelling house, hereditaments and messuage thereof, on an ominous day of thick, sulphurous, yellow light, when all the birds have stopped singing, and it is quite likely that an earthquake or a tempest, quite possibly followed by a flood, will do their dirty work for them. Or even if it's quite a nice day this may tempt one of the big stock

149

farmers in the wild frontier district where I live to drive a vast herd of two thousand bellowing cattle to the city.

He and his men, some on horseback and some in Land Rovers, are pretty inefficient and it's clear the day will not pass without Impact with any of the said Buildings by any Road Vehicle, Horses or Cattle . . . And that's only the Policy. They keep sending amendments enlarging this vast scenario. Aircraft. 'Other aerial devices *or articles dropped therefrom* are now included' they say (my italics). I take this to mean balloons, because I've often been in aircraft myself and I know for a fact it's impossible to drop any article from them, they won't let you open the window. So it must be balloons.

I shall hear this laughter and singing in the sky. I look up, and there is this bearded chap in a Norfolk jacket whooping it up with a champagne picnic with two girls who look like *cocottes* to me, although it's difficult to tell when they're a couple of hundred feet up in a balloon, and anyway I don't have much time to look because a champagne bottle—help, *three* champagne bottles—whistle down 'causing havoc to windows, doors, fanlights, greenhouses, conservatories and verandahs' and the 'fixed wash-basins, pedestals, sinks, lavatory pans and cisterns therein'.

It's a pretty extensive estate I've got there, I can tell you. Not everyone has pedestals and fixed washbasins or even lavatory pans in his greenhouses, but my insurance people are ready for it. In fact they know very well that no one could be more surprised than I was at inheriting it from this crazy old Great-aunt Philippa that I had. Naturally, I don't think she was crazy. It's true I used to sit for hours on the verandahs and in the said greenhouses reading from *Witherspoon on Regeneration* to her when she became an invalid, but I was the only one who didn't argue with her over her conviction that the BBC were trying to poison her, sending poisonous rays at her through the television.

It was a harmless delusion, and one that her son Reuben would have done well not to ridicule in that nasty

150

thin-lipped sneering way of his. He was furious when she left *me* the great house, with all these 'domestic offices, stables, garages and outbuildings' (not to mention all those lavishly equipped greenhouses); and I wouldn't be surprised if he isn't behind the Maoists on the lawn, although lately he's come right out into the open, yelling incoherent obscenities as he roams through the greenhouses with a sledgehammer. I got the police on to him of course, but it's a good job I had this amendment which said: 'Impact. Damage caused by members of the Insured's family not residing with him is now included . . .'

To tell the truth, I've never been used to living quite on this scale. One thing I've never understood quite about insuring one's household goods is whether they just accept the value *you* put on them. I wrote to them and the reply they sent, which I have pondered on for hours, sitting in one of the greenhouses that escaped Reuben on that memorable day, doesn't seem very helpful. They said:

. . . 'as far as the insurance valuation of a property is concerned, this has no direct bearing whatsoever on the value itself of the property. The insurance value is the cost from time to time to rebuild the property if it were destroyed . . . as far as the Contents Insurance is concerned, the loss is assessed at present day value of the articles lost (not replacement value).'

What's the difference? It I lost them I'd have to replace them, wouldn't I? I'm not ashamed to admit it, I feel a bit of a *nouveau riche* in Great-aunt Philippa's mansion. I've started buying a few antiques, and I've become aware from the catalogues of sales that the real gentry obviously live in houses stuffed with tallboys, smallboys, Samson bocage (whatever that is), majolica wall brackets in turquoise and dark blue, girandoles, nephrite paperweights, Fijian Lalis, Continental pierced comports, etc.

They know how much they're worth, whether for insurance or selling. They're always selling. 'What a charming pierced and embossed grape harvester's hod,' says a visitor over some very dry sherry; 'and I like that seascape of trading vessels in a heavy swell (18th century

Dutch school). But I don't think I've seen that boat group of eight immortals and a ho-ho bird, *signed on a rad label,* before.'

'O, Torquil and I thought it was time we went round the world again,' says the hostess, with a languid wave of her delicate blue-veined hand, 'so we're just getting a few things together for the auctioneer to pay for it.'

I don't have things like that, to sell or insure (and I always thought a girandole was a wild Provençal dance). Suppose I attempted to make the stuff I have got in my house sound impressive? Like this:

An early portable gramophone (no tone-arm) and a quantity of records by Jack Payne, Gracie Fields and others.

A number of pre-electric shaving devices, with *trois-trou* blades by Gillette and others.

A round-keyed *machine à écrire* with *rouge-et-noir* ribboning and stationary *sous-carriage,* the whole mounted on low rubber finials. (No letter M.)

A playroom pianoforte, with detachable side panels (47 silent notes) the interior garnished with marbles, *anciens biscuits* and *papiers des bon-bons.*

A 'Surprise' falling-down table, the fourth leg detached by Jennings the Younger.

A Gallimaufry of 177 mixed antique Shoes.

Would my insurance chaps be surprised by a list like that? I don't think so. There's every Chance they'd find it Predictable. You can't surprise insurance chaps.

CAMPING IT OUT

A camp bed is really a contradiction in terms. There are only *bedroom* beds, and anything alse is an unfruitful marriage between a camp sleeping-bag and some kind of dwarf bridge—like many real bridges, either trestle or cantilever.

The trestle kind is what other people always seem to have. I have never actually seen one in a shop. It seems to be like the Viscount, not manufactured for years now, but ubiquitous as ever, greeted with the same ambivalence between *reliable old thing* and, as one gets into it, *I hope this is going to be all right*. It has many stout wooden struts, and hinged pieces of black iron. When folded it looks like three old garden chairs and weighs like five; it can only have been intended for a camp that had pack-mules. We have a whole real divan that weighs less. When it opens everything happens at once, as with a conjuror's bunch of flowers or an umbrella. Indeed the canvas is generally shaped like two umbrellas up-ended. With slight adjustment it could probably be made into two officer's baths. These two hollows are separated by an iron cross-piece that sticks into the sleeper's hip.

If the sleeper tries to adjust this cross-piece in the night something goes *guk* and the bed collapses. In a room full of cupboards and shoes, under a high light, isolated in mad wakefulness from a sleeping world, the sleeper (for it is he) creeps about trying not to make clumping noises with the bed as he attacks a kind of three-dimensional intelligence test (how the hell did *they* put it up? They just seemed to pull one end, like this; *sqerr-k, erk, gromp, crash*). Even if he succeeds it has the madness of all utterly solitary acts (what's the use of passing an intelligence test if you can't tell anyone?), but usually he gives it up and lies at the bottom of a high, slack roll of canvas, unable to turn, as though in a rigid hammock, and with his hip on the floor. At least it is better than that cross-piece.

The cantilever kind is what you get when you actually buy a camp bed (the trestle kind are all inherited by people whose fathers were in Colonel Younghusband's expedition to Tibet in 1904). It is very thin and clever. Its two thin sides are supported by four thin lengths of steel in the shape of flattened Ws. When folded it looks like a broken golf umbrella. The idea is that the weight of the sleeper flattens the Ws some more, making them press the sides outwards and thereby keep the canvas flat. There is thus an unobstructed yielding surface large enough for the frantic twists and turns of true healthy sleep. These take the sleeper to the outlying edges of the bed which overhang the points of the W on which it rests, and the whole thing rolls over. It is thus necessary to sleep as rigid and unmoving as in the collapsed trestle bed.

As the trestle bed is monstrously heavy, so the cantilever bed is monstrously light. The trestle bed seems to get made up late at night, by three people laughing after a merry dinner; the cantilever bed, somehow, is always made up early in the day, before the expected sleeper has arrived; perhaps even the weight of bedclothes (tucked into nothing, as usual in camp beds) will stop it from blowing about in a draught. As it is, the bed moves about by itself and is always in a different position when you enter the room, so that one of the two ends of thin steel rod that stick out at the end catches you on the ankle again.

But the most likely reason for its early assembly is the difficulty of this operation. The cantilever camp bed illustrates the Third Law of Resistentialism (*unmanoeuvrability varies inversely with size*. In a constricted shed it is more difficult to turn a small wheelbarrow than a cumbersome bicycle almost twice the length. A motor scooter occupies up to four times the road and parking space, in relation to its size, that a car does. Little is known yet, but research already indicates that the mysterious 'awkwardness field', in some ways a repulsion force like the inverse of a magnetic field, is far more intense round small objects, such as fuses, plugs, razors, watches, fleas, than it is with large ones such as elephants, houses, large copper balls or town clocks with hourly processions of allegorical figures).

It requires an area three times as great as its own for assembly. It is folded in half. When it is unfolded and the two half-sections of the thin sides are being slotted together the unattached ends of the flattened W's flail about, knocking down clocks and lamps and becoming lodged in banisters. When the assembler (for it is he) kneels astride the first W to fit its other end into a lug on the thin side he cannot get this lug to point the right way; the Ws are all on the wrong side of the canvas. He must therefore turn the whole thing over. In the course of this operation the two halves come apart again. Then, kneeling again astride the upturned W he must seize the far end and pull it in with all his strength, at the same time accurately guiding this end into the lug and, with his third hand, stopping the lug from turning round. It is like simultaneously lifting a boulder and picking a daisy.

It is even harder to disassemble, since the weight of the sleeper has forced all joints into a tight fit. But, of course, it would probably all be easy in a camp.

PUTTING THE PIANO

In all the tremendous fuss about the Olympic Games every four years—the wrangling about venue, security, striking stadium-builders, amateur status, political bias, dope, the intermediate sex of Iron Curtain weight-lifters and shot-putters—not much thought seems to be given to the relevance of the events to actual modern life.

The *old* Olympic Games did have an obvious connection with what *was* then a fact of life; that those states did best whose citizen-soldiers were the fittest. When the semi-finals of the Peloponnesian War came round everybody stopped discussing truth and beauty under the marble columns and marched off, from Socrates downwards.

There was a half-heartred attempt at up-dating when the Games were revived by Baron Coubertin. The modern biathlon involves ski-ing for miles and still having a steady enough hand to be able to shoot someone—sorry, some *target*. It is usually won by some Swedish soldier from an army that has not been in battle since 1812, so you can tell how useful it is.

Surely what we need is an Olympics to set world standards of stamina, calm, control and resourcefulness in the actual situations of ordinary domestic life? Here are a few suggestions.

HOUSEHOLDER'S PENTATHLON (Male)

Involves five basic athletic skills; laying the carpet,

lifting the piano, screwing without gimlet, shop catching and domestic weightlifting. Competitors start in a room which contains a roll of carpet, exactly the width of the room, in which there is nothing else but a boudoir grand piano. First they must lay the carpet, finishing with the piano on the carpet.

Next they must get six 1¼ in wood screws through a side-piece of wood .8 inches thick into the ends of two shelves (i.e. three screws per shelf), using only a screwdriver (gimlet cannot be found, and this kind of thing is usually done late on Sunday afternoon when it is impossible to buy another one). 'Shop catching' means catching the shop open; it is assumed that an important fuse blows ten minutes before the nearest shop selling fuse wire (of which of course there is none in the house) closes. It is one mile away.

In the final event competitors are assumed to be halfway up a curved staircase with some awkwardly shaped object weighing 90 lb when the telephone rings.

HOUSEHOLDER'S PENTATHLON (Female)

Involves stepping the pram, weighing the dust, cooking the omelette, catching the shop and domestic weightlifting. In the first part the competitor must get a pram of standard dimensions, weighing with its contents 40 lb, up 30 steps, while carrying in the other arm a block weighing 25 lb (representing a second child), along a half-mile straight course with 30 kerbs, and down 30 steps at the other end. Then she must vacuum-clean the carpet area for 20 minutes (one point awarded for each gramme of dust in the bag; it is special, heavy dust, made of powdered rocks from Mount Olympus). At some point in the next part (cooking the omelette) a signal is given denoting that a *mobile* shop has arrived down the road. If she does not get to the shop (100 yards down the road) within 18 seconds it will have moved on a further 100 yards. She then completes the omelette. The domestic weightlifting is the same as in the male pentathlon except that the weight is reduced to 60 lb.

MOTORIST'S BIATHLON

A tough six-mile course. Each level one-mile section ends with a 100-yard stretch of gentle and slightly curved uphill gradient (1 in 25). Competitors must push a 1,000 cc car of a standard weight along the whole course. At the top of each gradient (on which they will of course have had to steer as well as push) they will have to assemble some delicate piece of mechanism, such as a carburettor or petrol pump, with small springs and set-screws (a severe test of muscular and nervous control) before starting the next section.

COMMUTER'S RACE

Competitors sprint 500 yards to 'own' station, assumed to be closed through shortage of staff, strike, engineering work, derailment or some other cause. They then run or (it is up to them) jog three miles to the 'next' station, also assumed to be their arrival station. Here the only escalator running is the down one; the others are blocked off because of shortage of staff, strike, engineering work, eruption of rogue jet of natural porridge from earth below, the occupation of the planet by spiders from Mars, or some other cause. After running up this down escalator they run half a mile to the 'office tower' where it is assumed they work on the 15th floor and the lifts are not working because the liftmen belong to the wrong union; they must therefore run up 400 steps.

BAGGAGE RACE

A special course of bridges, steps and tunnels, length 900 yards, over which competitors carry two bags, each weighing 35 lb. It is based on the real-life situation when a train due to leave from Platform 1 is re-announced from Platform 15 two-and-a-half minutes before departure. An early lead is almost vital on the starting open space, since passing becomes difficult thereafter, although ground can be made up on the final 100-yard sprint (as if train had started). Handicap points for over-60s.

SHED BUILDING RELAY RACE

For team of seven. First man runs 100 yards with floor, hands token to second man who runs back and fetches gable end, token to third man who fetches long wall, and so on till pitched-roof shed is erected.

THROWING THE SPONGE

Derived from situation when man washing his car sees cat scratching up vegetable bed he has just hoed and sown with various seeds, sponge is only missile to hand. It is, of course, much harder to throw a sponge than a stone. Especially a *dry* sponge. In early days of this event there are scandals involving use of drugs which make palms moist so that sponge is slightly wetted and more throwable, but dope tests are soon introduced.

LAWNMOWER RACE

With grassboxes on, 1000 metre (one lap) course, with fortnight's summer growth. Competitors must run to grass heap in centre of field every time box is full.

You can imagine the excited commentator: 'Oh, this is a fantastic end to a great race. There's S. Alexandrov, who already is ahead for the course on his previous Olympic record of 2.5432 minutes, fighting to hold off Britain's Harry Tubbs, the unknown Carshalton bank cashier. Unbelievably, Tubbs is inching ahead. Oh, my word, what superb fitness! The grass is flying into the boxes. Ten metres to go! The crowd are on their feet— he's, yes, he's *done* it, an incredible two minutes 40 seconds! Harry Tubbs wins the Lawnmower Race for Britain, the original home of the sport which has for so long been dominated by Russia and America! Well, there'll be dancing in the streets of Carshalton tonight . . .'

And that is not all. Back in Russia lawnmower-racing has opened people's eyes to the pleasure of having a garden of one's own; people want their own lawns, perhaps even one day their own houses, the freedom to buy, sell, move from one place to another . . .

Well, we can dream, can't we? After all, Baron Coubertin did.

DEAR ELECTRICITY BOARD
....

Dear Electricty Board,

As you may know, our storage heater has failed. Well, perhaps you *don't know,* perhaps the girl who answered the three times I phoned you last week has left to get married, and forgot to tell you, in all the happy confusion of the office party, the presentation and so on. Anyway, as I haven't heard anything from you I thought I'd write.

There is something very wrong inside the heater itself. It isn't just the fuse. That was the first thing your girl asked me. As I told her, when I put a new fuse in and switch on, it emits a bright blue flash and a sound best spelt, I think, *kerspluck*.

A short, in short. Sorry about that; but it would be pointless for you to think you are dealing with a household where there is no technical knowledge of electricity at all. In these days of staff and other shortages I am sure you would not want to send a maintenance man on a round journey of 30 miles just to change a fuse.

However, I hope all your maintenance men have not left to get married as well, and that you will pass on to the one that eventually comes the contents of this letter. Then he will know what spare parts to bring.

It might also, perhaps, be shown to your design department, because I have discovered a fault in your storage heaters which you perhaps do not know about and may wish to rectify in future models. It is this: your storage heaters are not mouse-proof.

I am not saying the mouse caused the short. We only got the short last week (the mouse was two months ago), when my younger son sat on the end of the heater to watch the television, as he often does when none of my daughters are sitting on it for the same purpose (and sometimes when they are, since he is stronger).

The reason the heater collapsed when my younger son sat on it was that my elder son (who is 21 and knows much more about electricity than even I do, as you will presently see) must have left out some purely mechanical part of the structure at one end when he re-assembled it after getting the mouse out, two months ago. When my younger son sat on it (last week) there was a sudden noise best spelt, I think, GAK, and this end (the end facing the television) was suddenly four inches lower than the other end. Some sort of leg or support had evidently not been properly secured.

Now you will doubtless say that my elder son had no business, however much he knows about electricity, dismantling one of your storage heaters. But I must point out that he only did this after you had sent no one in response to the calls I had made about the mouse.

In these calls, I told (I imagine) another girl who also left to get married and is probably back from the honeymoon by now, about the *smell*. Your heater, as I said, not being mouse-proof, a mouse had got into it. Arriving at a part no doubt warmer than the bit my children sit on to watch television, it had then, finding it *too* warm, discovered that it was easier to get in than out. And so it died, right in there.

Perhaps you do not realise how much smell a dead mouse can give off. Probably this smell is worse when the process of decomposition is speeded up by the surrounding heat.

You must remember that this was the most lived-in room in the house. The room with the TV in it, for Pete's sake, and the room we eat in. Even so, we had almost got used to it, as one does, when my elder son came home for a weekend from college, where he is doing science (I told you he knows all about electricity).

Coming straight from a fresher atmosphere, he found the smell intolerable. What finally decided him to have a go (and I am bound to tell you that my objection was by now very lukewarm) was that *another* mouse had got inside, that very day. We could hear it scuttling about. It must

160

have known there was a dead comrade in there, but this did not seem to deter it. But then mice do not have our deductive minds, do they? Of course it may have been a heroic rescue mouse, or perhaps the loyal mate of the dead one; but this is mere speculation.

As I do not need to tell *you,* there is nothing very complicated electrically about a storage heater. Neither of us was very surprised, when we had finally lifted the casing off, to find just a lot of heavy concrete blocks, with grooves through which ran a long spiral element, and a great deal of stuff that looked to me like horsehair, although I don't doubt that in these scientific days, it is in fact some man-made material.

Our main trouble, as you will guess, was the purely mechanical one of getting the casing off. The four bottom screws at the sides were comparatively easy. It was the brackets fixing the blas...—the heater to the wall. I have since rejected as fanciful the only explanation that seemed possible at the time—that *these* screws were put in by dwarfs or mannikins only two inches tall, but possessed of superhuman strength.

At any rate I shall be interested, when your man finally comes, to see what kind of tool can screw a screw so darn tight when the head of the screw is three inches away from a wall, at the bottom of a heavy and immovable object. The bracket itself is, as you know, apparently now a fixed part of the house.

We did get the casing off in the end, with what my son described as necessary and legitimate wrenching.

'It will go on again all right,' he said, and so it proved, some time after we had got the mouse out. This, as you may imagine, was a laborious process, involving the removal of the concrete blocks layer by layer (I was quite right, they *do* get hotter as one gets lower) and keeping the yards of element untangled.

We found the dead mouse, and we could hear the live one scuttling about as we came nearer ground level, like harvesters pushing rabbits into an ever-decreasing circle of uncut corn.

We were waiting not with guns, of course, but with our cat. However, she took a minimal interest in the proceedings, and when we actually put her on what was left of the heater and told her to do her stuff she jumped away very angrily. We must be among the very few people who have ever actually seen a cat on hot bricks.

We are probably among the few, also, to have caught a mouse with a dustpan and brush, for this is what we used when it emerged from under the very last block and ran into a corner. We put it back in the garden, hoping against hope that it would tell the other mice to keep the hell out of it.

By the time we had cleared up the unbelievable mess of half-dried jam, half-eaten sweets, crumbs and crisps from that normally unreachable bit of floor (to a mouse it must have seemed like a marvellous Harrods' Food Hall where everything is free, as well as offering heated beds upstairs) and carefully reassembled the heater, it was time for my elder son to go back to college.

The casing, as he had predicted, did go on again all right, although one or two of the screws did not seem to be screwing *into* anything, and it rattled a bit if you hit it.

Most of all, it still *worked*. For two months, and without that smell. We put (and here is a free idea for your design department) a guard round the bottom, of chicken-wire. Well, mouse-wire I suppose you would call it really.

And now this. One end sort of collapsed, a dead short somewhere inside, muffled figures in blankets watching the television. A dead mouse we felt was in our province, but a dead short is surely in yours.

Do please send someone fairly quickly.

Yours faithfully,

Paul Jennings.

LOVE A DUCK? WHATEVER FOR?

If any of your friends keep ducks, and you have any children, sooner or later these friends will invite you to tea on a nice summery day, and on their little pond with the weeping willow there will be a charming sight; a duck, a drake, and eight or nine ducklings, enchanting little fluffy aquatic oranges skittering across the water after them.

Your friends probably won't tell you that this is only the second day the ducklings have been considered big enough to be able to get away from the drake when he tries to eat them. They won't tell you they had to build a second duck-house, somewhere out of sight, where they had to put him while the duck (or ducks, for drakes are, to put it mildly, polygamous) were sitting, to stop him from treading on the eggs accidentally on purpose and eating *them*.

They won't tell you a lot of things. They will exchange glances as your children cry, 'Oh, could we really have some, *please*?' Well, after eight years I am now, thank heaven, an ex-duck-keeper. I can tell you what is behind those glances.

It is very difficult to love ducks.

Ducklings, yes. But not ducks. I'm sure I now understand the origin of that expressive Cockneyism 'Lor love a duck!' Love a duck? You must be joking.

This is not to say I hated them. It is impossible to establish any kind of relationship with ducks, whether of love or hate. No matter how much I did for them or how nicely I talked to them (though not going as far as my wife, who somehow got it into her head that you say *gisha* to ducks; 'gisha, gisha, come on duckies!') it was no go.

Even when I came with great bags of food, they would flap away going WAAAAAK, just as If I were any old farmer about to wring their necks. As I walked away the drake would come after me, his beak fiercely lowered, to impress his wives, but if I turned suddenly he would pretend it wasn't him at all.

Ducks keep escaping, especially when your lettuces are coming up. They can erode any known form of bark, nibble nabble nibble all day long with their beaks. If there were ducks on the Thames the Houses of Parliament would fall into it inside ten years.

Above all, unless you keep them purely as potential

163

dinners (like some other friends of ours; 'would you care for a piece of Henry?', the husband said to us, his carving knife poised . Quite put us off, it did, we'd been talking to Henry the week before), ducks seem to get into all the chinks of your life, like pets, except they don't *act* like pets. They just absorb time, money and thought without giving anything back, unless you count about twelve eggs each early summer, which was all we got. Duck eggs are too gooey to eat, so we put them in cake, and even that was gooey and nobody like it much.

Our friends (not the ones with Henry, just some friends who were, I now see, half-way along the road to disillusion with ducks-as-pets which I have now trodden) offered us three ducklings, the children having promised solemnly to feed them. I should have got that in writing for a start. *I, Susanna, hereby undertake to feed the ducks on Mondays. I, Edward, hereby undertake to feed the ducks on Tuesdays. I, Matthew . . .*

We couldn't take them straight away because we hadn't got a duckpond to put them on. Well, who has? I said we would come back in a fortnight, after I had made one. Ha.

It took the next four weekends, and a lot of evenings as well, and a lot of hot baths and liniment. It seemed simple enough in theory. A ditch runs past the bottom of the garden. I would dig a pit, eighteen inches deep, ten feet by ten feet, on the garden side of this ditch, leaving a thin wall of soil to be knocked down at the last moment to let the water in.

I had only got twelve inches down by the second weekend. I had forgotten that you can't dig down three inches in our garden, let alone eighteen, without coming to tree roots and suckers. It's like the Matto Grosso. At twelve inches it was an intricate network of tough, whippy roots as thick as your arm. I had to lay aside the spade for the axe half the time.

On one of the few nights when I wasn't toiling away there, my son Edward discovered that by knocking down the thin wall he could let the water in *now*. In spite of attempts to rebuild the wall and to bale or siphon the water

164

out, I spent the rest of the time standing in mud, hacking at tree roots and often missing because at the last moment I had to avert my face from the great mud-splat. It was about this time, too, that I discovered that size 8 gumboots are only twelve inches high, if that.

When we brought the ducklings home. . . .

Oh, I nearly forgot; when I had made the duckpond I had to enclose it. Stakes, £8. Strong wire netting, £7. hinges and stuff for gate, £3. Duckhouse (even a smelly, secondhand one), £5. That was £23, eight years ago, it would be a lot more now, even if you just happened to know someone with a secondhand duckhouse.

This involved a lot *more* digging, and some new problems. For instance, the thing about wire netting is that however well you align your stakes, the top of the netting is longer than the bottom, or vice versa. Either way, you have to take in a sort of tuck in the longer end at each stake, to keep the stuff anywhere near rigid . . .

Well, when we brought the ducklings home at last, they were already past their pristine charm. That's all nonsense about ugly ducklings, it's only later that they get ugly. We had a drake and two ducks, because there is no male chauvinist like a drake.

It was clear from the start that he had a favourite wife, so we called them William and Mary. The third one, who always got elbowed, or rather winged, away from any food that was going, was one of nature's Jemima's, so that is what we called her. I can't say we loved her (still less that she loved us) but at least we felt sorry for her. Sometimes, when she looked particularly scraggy and overworked, we would hold William and Mary off while she hastily gobbled what she could, as they muttered duck curses at us.

After a month it was less bother to take the food down ourselves than endlessly remind the children of their promise. In no time it was winter. Often angry WAAAAK sounds would remind us that no one had fed the ducks. Susanna at dancing class, Matthew doing his homework for once, let's not interrupt *that,* Edward would fall over and drop the bucket so we would go out with bucket and torch through the rainy darkness down to the appalling, slippery, muddy slum they had made round their pond.

The food consisted of kitchen scraps and some stuff our friends said they had to have, called Layers' Mash, which seemed to be a mixture of sand and barley husks and cost £2 for 56 pounds, which lasted two months, so that was £12 a year. It was only after six years that we discovered that they laid exactly the same number of eggs (about twelve, each early summer, you remember) with only the kitchen scraps. So that was £72 worth of Layers' Mash, plus the original £23, making £95 in all. Rather a lot for one gooey cake which nobody liked very much.

We only made this one cake, at the end of the first year, because of two developments in the second year. Catch A was that we discovered, rather late in the day, that the ditch dried up in the summer, or at any rate wasn't high enough to flow into the silted-up pond. This left the ducks with 100 square feet of green mud, which had to be excavated all over again before we could fill the pond with the garden hose. And refill it. And refill it . . .

I read an article which said that eggs laid by ducks who did not have running water were not safe; there was a danger of *botulism,* a dreadful-sounding version of ptomaine poisoning.

We had enough on our hands, never mind botulism, with Catch B; ducks are *escapologists.* With their endless nibble-nabble they soon pushed out the edges of their pond; first so that they could escape via the ditch, and later, as the stakes and netting collapsed inwards, and the gate fell apart, and the whole sordid enclosure became a thing, in Shakespeare's words, of looped and window'd raggedness, so that they could escape at almost any point.

Sometimes they escaped to the lettuces.

Sometimes, when the pond was dry, they escaped to a tiny ornamental fountain on the lawn, filling it with feathers (ducks are *always* moulting) and the green mud they brought with them.

Sometimes Mary and Jemima would escape into the field on the other side of the ditch to lay their eggs where they hoped William wouldn't find them. In fact finding the eggs was always a kind of Easter Sunday race between us and William. It was, needless to say, Jemima who attempted actual sitting now and again, when she thought the others weren't looking. Over the eight years we got four duck-lings, that we actually saw: but none of them survived.

The one place they wouldn't escape to was a beautiful, big, proper duckpond that has been in the field at least since 1752, according to an old map, and never dries up. On many a hot summer day we would form a line of beaters behind them, even the children helping for once, my wife crying 'Gisha, duckies, look! Lovely water!'

And every time, they would evade us, William and Mary together as they rushed into impenetrable nettle-beds and brambles, Jemima WAAAAAKing fit to bust somewhere else, separated from them. We would go back into the house, and after a suitable interval they would come waddling back to the fountain with the mindless determina-tion of Daleks.

In the end we simply gave them away to a farmer. A month later we had the ultimate proof (Catch C if you want pets with a scrap of intelligence); *ducks are unpredictable idiots*. Haunted by vague memories of the kitchen scraps and the lettuces and the fountain, they escaped from the farmer, and went straight back to the pond in the field which they had hitherto avoided. They made no attempt to get in touch with us; their brains, if that is what ducks have, couldn't cope with the last step.

I have filled in our pond, and put the netting right across the end of the garden, just in case, though. I'm an ex-duck-keeper now, and I intend to stay that way.

HOW MUCH IS THAT COLLABRADOR IN THE WINDOW?

When I look at thoroughbred dogs, even that splendidly-named Burlington Bossy-boots, that won at Crufts last year, I never wish they were mine, any more than I wish I was married to Miss Earth or the Deb of the Year.

The fact is, breeding and competition-winning lead to a cul-de-sac of exquisite uselessness. The aristocrat began by being better at some function than his rivals; whether it was knocking other men off their horses in battle or, in the case of dogs, fetching snipe, or killing other dogs, or whatever.

But that is not what the judges at dog shows are thinking about as they peer at the exhibits. They are looking to see whether the creature is dish-faced, bench-legged: same as fiddle-front, or east-west; cloddy; stoutly built; sickle-hocked or out at elbow. They want to see if they can knock off any marks for cat foot, pig eye, dudley nose: flesh-coloured, apple head or maybe just poor front or wet neck. I am not making all this up, it is in *The Encyclopaedia of Dog Breeds* by Ernest B. Hart, and other similar books.

But I like dogs to be out at elbow. It gives me a fellow-feeling with them. It does not do dogs any more good than people to be bred to some abstract specification of points. This is tacitly recognised in the case of people. Miss Earth may have the perfect vital statistics and be able to read simple words. The Deb of the Year may have that mysterious quality of merry vacuity that attracts gossip columnists; but then she gets involved with a lorry driver or pop singer to revitalise the strain, or Miss Earth goes on to get A-levels or something.

Dog aristocrats are not allowed to do this. No wonder that among the faults of a breed called Weimaraner are listed 'doggy bitches and bitchy dogs'. I detect a note of wistfulness in the official qualities expected when it comes to marks for 'temperament'. A Springer, it says should look 'alert, kindly and trusting,' whereas an Afghan should be 'aloof and dignified, yet gay'. You cannot get *people* like that, let alone dogs.

I do not doubt that some of the champions, especially the poodles, are very clever. We were probably unlucky with our three dogs, which have all been thoroughbreds and thoroughstupids into the bargain.

We began with a Sealyham that had a long pedigree. Its uncle was Princess Margaret's dog. It was beautiful to look at, not cloddy or dish-faced; and perhaps would still have been good at killing polecats or foulemarts, which is what this breed was originally developed for. But we have not got any foulemarts.

And another dog, called Bates (we also had a cat called Elliot at the same time, so that we could get away from boring parties saying that Bates and Elliot were waiting for us; people would think it was the butler and the maid), was unbelievably and, apparently, incurably stupid.

Most people get it into a puppy's head after six months or so that there is a difference between inside and outside and that certain things are best done outside. The nearest we ever got to success with Bates was that when he was outside he would make a special point of coming inside to do it.

He kept running away, not because he did not like us but because he was too stupid to be able to tell the difference between us and anyone else, or between our house and any other house. It was either give him away or put up about 600 yd. of chain-link fencing, so we gave him away. Besides, he ate chair legs.

Then we had a Spaniel, called Barker, who thought he was a mole, or possibly an Australian, and that digging time it rang he set up a dismal howl which made conversation impossible. He had a colossal pedigree too, with ancestors called Silver Sky of Ulwell, Bretlyn Glencora Gaycount and even Weston Flamethrower of Bradfield.

He had some fearful aristocratic disease of the ear, like the haemophilia of the Spanish royal family; not the ordinary Spaniel ear trouble, but some very obscure thing, which was investigated by men in white coats in Cambridge.

Our present dog, the grand-nephew of this Barker, is a sex maniac, throwback to some dissolute 18th century rake in the line; he does not mind who the partner is, whether his own grandfather or a Labrador four times as big as

169

himself. When not so engaged he wanders round the canine equivalent of coffee-houses in the village, lost in lecherous thought, usually in the middle of the road, with the result that he has been mildly run over three times.

But he has drawn no deduction from this, he just lurches back to the house and flops down in a good wicker chair which he has taken over. He would not take the slightest notice, in his coma, if an unshaven man in striped jersey and black mask, carrying a sack labelled SWAG, started climbing in through the kitchen window. And he eats window-frames.

We are not the only ones, either. A friend of ours had a pedigree Great Dane which one day rushed out at a Mini in which his wife's mother was arriving and did what turned out to be £60 worth of damage to it; and when she got out it knocked her down and broke her leg.

Some friends had a very grand dog called an Abyssinian Lion Ridgeback or some such name, and a pedigree spaniel. They lived together amicably enough, and when they went into kennels during the family's holiday the kennel-owner naturally put them in together. On the second morning she found the Ridgeback had eaten the spaniel.

That is what breeding in an artificial urban civilisation has led to; dogs of so high and inbred a class that we have been so busy worrying about their hocks, stifles, flags, flews, feathers and the rest of it that we have not noticed that many of them are now actually crazy.

It is significant that it was in Africa, one notices, in *Dogs of the World* by Dr Erich Schneider-Meyer, that an Englishman developed an apparently officially recognised breed: the Sealydale. And you'll never believe what the German for Great Dane is . . . Deutsche Dogge.

The Sealydale: 'about 12 in. high, neck long and strong, body long-cast' obviously came about because on some lonely farm they had a Sealyham dog and an Airedale bitch. If it had been the other way round they would have had an Airyham: 24 in. high, high stifles, built rather like the Trojan Horse, able both to drive off wild African

170

hyenas *and* deal with foulemarts when its owners came home on leave.

It suggests a whole new range of classifications by which Crufts and the Kennel Club could revitalise the whole thing without resorting to the canine equivalent of the debutante living with the lorry driver: the Poodale, the Terrioodle, the Dachter, the Peagle, the Small Dane, the Alsaluki, the Labraniel, the Long-haired Spandle, the old Irish Hellhound, the Bazooka, the Collabrador. . . .

If dog breeders set their sights on the right objective, they would, instead of looking to an ever more dried-up future, look beyond the mists of the past; beyond the time when Darwinian processes had already produced natural territorial differences; the Alaskan Malamute with its thick fur, the Mexican Hairless for all that hot weather near the Equator, the Crab-eating Dog, *Canis cancrivorus,* the Norwich Terrier for Norwich people, to the basic, original creature, which we now tend to call Mongrel—the pure Platonic Form of dog.

At present there are scoring systems, in which points are awarded for head, body, running gear (legs to you), coat, tail, general appearance, temperament. If my recommendation were adopted, how marvellously the vocabulary for the points and faults would be revitalised, as well as the stock itself!

The best mongrel in the show would have a *bruffy* bark: not a high yap, not a ferocious baying, but—well, bruffy. He would have a *self-righting coat:* after swimming he would be bone dry after about three minutes, not going along on one ear on the carpet saying *grrrrrooooooo* two hours afterwards like our pedigree spaniel. He would almost certainly be *barby:* having a beard; and the judges would check to see that he *lolloped* properly; with his running gear, of course.

He would gain points for *twinkle* and *bounce* and *multiples* (incorporation of the maximum number of points taken at random from other breeds—long tail, pointed ears, long front legs and short back ones, perhaps even one pointed ear and one rounded one). He would be penalised for *pin-head:* not wide enough to leave room for any brains; *yap, shiver, pedigree glaze* (or *dope-eye*), a fault of over-breeding.

It would be a long time before they bred dogs like *that* so successfully that they could not tell the difference between the baker and the burglar. Ours can't.

RUPTURED COMMUNICATIONS

Only people who have never had an operation will realise how heroic it is of me, asked to write an article for a medical journal when I have just had a hernia operation, not to write about *that*.

No, I shan't be referring to that at all. This article, in fact, is about the curious changes in the *names* of all the ills that flesh is heir to. Hernia is a case in point, it's a word that has come up in the last twenty years. Of course doctors knew it all along, but to laymen like me it used to be a *rupture*. Indeed, to a lot of people it still *is* a rupture. This man at the hospital was saying to everyone that he had 'a ruptured hernia'.

But hernia sounds altogether more medical, respectable. Once there's a proper Latin name for anything there's a feeling that the doctors know more about it (of course rupture is from a Latin root, too, it comes from *rumpere* 'to break, burst, tear, rend, rive, break asunder, force open' says my dictionary, isn't it marvellous of me not to say anything more about the operation, but those words give you the sketch, don't they?) Hernia sounds altogether more medical than rupture, which is part of everyday speech. *'Rupture between* EEC *partners', 'Left-wing union rupture',* one reads in the headlines, and one couldn't substitute the word hernia, much as one sometimes feels it would do them a power of good to shut up squabbling for a bit, and be shaved all over, and get into this backless operation gown, and have this pre-med pill (as we call it) and . . .

For years one of my favourite word-lists has been one

172

headed 'London's Weekly Bill of Mortality' which was in *The Reading Mercury* in 1757:

Abortive	2	Dropsie	25
Aged	45	Evil	1
Apoplexy	2	Fever	63
Asthma	1	Gout	1
Childbed	4	Grief	2
Griping in		Rising of the Lights	2
the guts	23	Small-pox	56
Chrisms	2	Stillborn	25
Headmould-Shot	4	Stoppage in the Stomach	3
Jaundies	6	Suddenly	1
Imposthume	2	Teeth	76
Livergrown	2	Tissic	8
Looseness	7	Thrush	3
Measles	6	Vomiting	1
Palsie	2	Water in the Head	3
Purples	1	Consumption	60
Mortification	1	Convulsion	308
Rickets	4		

Death, as somebody or other said is nature's warning to us to slow down, and it always has been. Obviously we've found the proper names for a lot of these things and know how to cure them. You don't hear people saying: 'Did you hear about poor old Jim, rushed off to hospital last Thursday with Thrush, they operated the same day?' Or, 'Sad about Mrs Smith, wasn't it? But of course Teeth ran in the family.'

I should like to have thought, 'posthumous' meaning 'after death', the 'Imposthume' meant the opposite, 'not after death', and that these were happy cases where the patient had actually been pronounced dead by the imperfect standards of those days (no breath showing on a mirror) and had then suddenly sat up again, like the dying miser in old farces; but on looking it up I find it's an old word for an abscess.

I'm not quite sure that we are as rid of some of these things as we think. I'm pretty sure I had a touch of Rising of the Lights in '57, and I know several people who've had (and some who've never been cured of) Evil. (And could Headmould-shot have been Brain Fever?)

The main thing that strikes you about this list is its Anglo-Saxon sense of physical reality, of the *body* as opposed to the Latinised abstractions of today's nomenclature. Having a body is a characteristic we share with the animals, and there is quite a resemblance between that list and another one I have, of the diseases of sheep. You wouldn't believe how many things sheep can get: Black Disease, Bradsot, Blow-fly Strike, Felon, Ganger, Grass-ill, Loss of Hair, Louping-ill, Maggot-fly Strike, Orf, Outburst, Pine, Pulpy Kidney Disease, Quarter-ill or Evil (ah *ha*! you see? *Evil*), Sheep Thrush, Staggers, Struck, Swayback, The Jumps, Trembles, Turnip Sickness, Vinquish, Wool on the Stomach, to name a few.

Now before we separate man completely from the rest of the animal creation and begin to think that all illness is in the mind, let this marvellously physical, un-Latin list give us pause, let us recognise that even in the days of dialysis machines, streptomycin, and all the other marvels, there are still mysterious, unclassifiable afflictions best described in common-speech terms; all we need is a bit of up-dating. Thus:

HOUSEWIFE'S NOD: Affication of middle-aged or young females, who nod and smile endlessly, sometimes uttering a few inane words, at detergent salesmen.

BLUES: Probably the same as 18-century *Purples,* but more lethargic symptoms.

WEEPING IN THE CONCRETE: Sensations of acute nausea, usually experienced in the open air, or what is left of it, in new 'shopping precincts', followed by uncontrolled weeping.

THE SNATCHES: Also known in higher (wine-drinking) circles as

TILLFINGER: Dissociation of arm and hand from rest of body, sufferer has no control over them.

174

STRIKE: Commonest disease of 20th-century England. Probably caught from sheep.

THE PEEPS: Uncontrollable desire to observe nude stage performances. Was once confined to middle-aged impotent men but now seems to afflict all age-groups.

SWAPPING OF THE WIFE: Last stage of the peeps, leading to

SEXMOULDSHOT: Total staring vacuity, with sudden violent intervals, smashing windows, jumping off cliffs, murdering girls in lanes, dying, etc.

HORNFINGER: A nervous disease of motorists.

AD NAUSEAM: A children's disease, in which they incessantly spoon up whatever product is placed before them, pausing only to stare straight ahead (at the camera), uttering gibberish words such as *yumyum* and baring their teeth in a fixed, uncontrollable grin or rictus.

UNBENDS: Not to be confused with the BENDS, suffered by divers when pressure is changed too abruptly. The UNBENDS is a special form of catatonic rigidity to which politicians are especially liable, especially prime ministers and union leaders.

RUPTURE: An injury often sustained by active, intelligent men. Usually it involves an extrusion of a portion of the contents of the abdominal cavity. Nowadays it is very often called a HERNIA and it can be successfully treated in an operation where, well, you go into hospital a couple of days before they actually do it, you have these routine tests, and of course you have to be shaved all over, and then on the day itself . . .

But I promised I wouldn't, didn't I?

SPECTACLES FOR GODS

You'll never believe this, but I was once in a room with 400 opticians all laughing. I was speaking at an opticians' dinner, I forget why now. I read a bit from a catalogue issued by a firm described as 'Government Surplus Clothiers'.

'Genuine POLICE MELTON CLOTH CAPES. Made in the Best Melton Cloth. Water repellent. Warm and handy. Suitable for opticians, etc.'

Well, they roared. It was one of the merriest dinners I've ever been to. I told the top optician, the chairman of the dinner, that I should have to rush off before the end; I dare not miss the last train because my wife was expecting a baby. He asked if it was the first. No, I said, the third.

'Don't have a fourth, will you?'

'Why not?'

'Well, you know that every fourth child born into the world is Chinese.'

That's what opticians are like underneath. Laughing, convivial men, with a quip for every occasion.

Not surprising, when you come to think of it. They must feel a need to react against the solemn quiet of those little cubicles where they deal all day long with a stream of people gloomily aware that they are not perfect human beings, and are getting less perfect all the time.

No one likes having glasses. Go into any art gallery. Look (if you've brought the right glasses with you) at all those gods and goddesses, those heavenly landscapes where all is joy and life, an artist's dream of the ideal. Do you see any figure wearing glasses? Not on your life. Can you imagine Alexander the Great, or Venus, or Napoleon, or an angel, or Beethoven, wearing glasses?

Actually Beethoven did wear them sometimes. Schubert wore them all the time. But I've got three little busts, of Beethoven, Schubert and Mozart, none of them with glasses. It so happens that these busts are made of soap—a Christmas present two years ago from one of my children. I have never used them (I should feel a bit of a Philistine washing with Mozart, watching him get less like Mozart and more like any other piece of soap every day). But it would have been quite easy to put soap glasses on these figures. It's not difficult technically. It is just that even soap makers recognise instinctively that glasses somehow reduce a man.

Opticians know that inside the middle-aged man who sits in that chair trying, without much enthusiasm, to decide whether a capital H with a red neon cross-piece, or one with two vertical bluish-green snakes, is a better approximation to the perfectly ordinary black one he knows to be there, there is a Greek god who dances all night and is a champion water-skier who can see for miles *and* read small print.

The man knows that he will come out of that cubicle yet one step farther away from his golden clear-sighted youth. Maybe he starts before he is middle-aged. He finds he needs glasses just for reading. The optician tells him he has *presbyopia*—and, like a fool, he looks it up in the dictionary.

He finds it is derived from the Greek *presbus*. It means *old man*. He is maybe 38. The optician says those funny-looking half-glasses are good for presbyopia. But it seems to the man that even Tarzan wearing those things would look like an old sheep.

Also he has an obscure feeling that they would be *draughty*. One's eyes are, so to speak, indoors behind proper glasses. Surely these sheep's-eye half-glasses will actually funnel wind into his eyes, making them water so that he looks older than ever?

Actually, whatever kind he chooses, after a year or so his eyes when he takes them off will have a defenceless, watery look about them anyway. Men in films are always taking the glasses off some rather dowdy secretary and saying, 'Do you realise you're beautiful without those glasses?' So she is. But that is only because she's a film star that Make-up has just spent two hours making dowdy. Really she is a beautiful water-skier, with 6/6 vision, whatever that means, in each eye, and she's just wearing prop frames with plain glass in them.

But nobody ever says to a man, 'Do you realise you're handsome without those glasses?' because they know darn well that without them he just looks like a man who ought to see an optician.

So the man has an ordinary pair of glasses, in so far as any glasses are ordinary. For the optician, knowing that the man has now been forced to abandon this dream of himself as a water-skiing Greek god, has a showcase of frames all of which pander to other dreams. If the man cannot be a handsome water-skier any more, perhaps he would care to be one of these:

Scholar—A successful scholar at that, because his glasses are all gold. Thin, wiry—but gold. The glasses of a kindly, rather withdrawn chap, who has spent years over his books, not going out much. But all the time his reputation has been quietly spreading. His publishers ask him respectfully how Volume IV is coming along: and hope he won't mind if they enclose this little cheque for £7,500. So he goes out and buys some more gold glasses. With a very slight alteration these frames could also belong to the:

First Violin in World-famous Quartet—A comfortable, loveable teddy-bear of a man . . . but a genius. The glasses slip forward on his nose when he leans forward to pencil a note in the score. See, in the melting slow movement a beautiful woman leans forward, lips parted, lost in ecstasy at his beautiful tone. She has been taken to the concert, with ulterior motives, by a:

Captain of Industry—He has massive black frames, with very thick side-pieces. They go with his big office, empty save for a big desk with an onyx pen-set and an intercom, on which he flips a switch with the well-manicured index-finger of one of his big hands. 'Get me Wither-spoon,' he rasps. This might well be the:

Company Secretary (Nasty)—He has cold eyes, to begin with, but they look even colder behind these rimless glasses, which are oblong, with another little straight edge at each corner; making eight sides in all. Suits him: he's an eight-sided man, none of them sides you would want to know. If there is any dirty work going on in the take-over field there will very likely be conversations on the phone between him and the:

Sinister Foreigner—It is impossible to see *his* eyes at all behind these monstrous pebble glasses, as he nods and murmurs 'Ah so. I think perhaps you vill co-operate efter all?' Quite different from the:

Company Secretary (Nice)—His glasses have a black piece across the tops of the oval lenses, which are rimless underneath. He has worked hard at evening classes, and has a home with wall-to-wall carpeting and 2.4 children. On Friday evenings he rehearses with an amateur dramatic society, where he could almost be mistaken for the:

Trustworthy Insurance Agent—The difference is that you never see this man in profile. He is always advancing towards you, ready with a firm handshake, looking straight at you with a frank, open expression. Again, there's not much difference between his glasses and those of the:

Twinkling Bank Manager—except that he's older, of course, and the black pieces at the top are thicker. He has more than a frank open expression, he has a frank open *smile*.

Nine times out of ten the man doesn't want to be any of these; but is obliged to settle for one of the last three, unless he happens to fancy himself as a:

Naturalist/Forester—A silent, shy man, only really happy among books or trees. His glasses have steel sides and round steel rims. They go well with his weatherbeaten face and the tall, stooping figure, clad in fading khaki shorts and carrying a complicated rucksack. And that only leaves:

Scrooge—Glaring myopically (not to mention presbyopically) at the world over crabby pince-nez.

If the man already used glasses for reading before he was this dotard of 38, he is quite likely to find, by the time he is 40, that even though he could use one of his lenses to light a cigarette from the sun, they are now no longer strong enough for reading. The optician gives him some new reading ones, with which he could probably set his book on fire with *either* lens. The old reading glasses now turn out to be just right for driving (managed with none at all till now, to the ill-concealed astonishment of the optician). So now he has two pairs.

Why not have bi-focals, the optician says next time,

179

surveying the man's scratched and twisted glasses held together with paperclips and fuse wire. But at this the last vestige of the water-skiing Greek god protests. Bi-focals! Time enough for that when the man is sitting up in bed with a shawl round his shoulders, sipping a little thin gruel, whatever that is.

So the optician fits him with yet stronger reading glasses. The recent reading glasses become the new driving glasses. The old driving glasses are now no use for anything, except perhaps lighting cigarettes on a hot day. No wonder opticians laugh when they are together.

DON'T DO IT YOURSELF, YOU FOOL

I have a theory about the immense popularity of Do It Yourself shops. I believe that today, just as before any of these shops existed, the only people who can make one end of a piece of ceiling paper stay up long enough for them to stick the other end without the whole thing flopping back on to their heads are men who have served a five-year apprenticeship with a builder and decorator.

I don't believe that the hordes of people in DIY shops buying those roller things are any better than I am at getting a patterned wallpaper round an uneven chimney breast. I believe they go there as a natural reaction to the modern manufacturer's policy, which is the exact opposite of DIY. Absolutely everything you buy nowadays is a Leave It Alone, or LIA product.

They are determined to deny us the simplest capacity for maintenance, emergency treatment or replacement of parts.

Take cars, for instance. In the first car I had, if I wanted to change a headlight bulb all I had to do was press the rim, give it a small anti-clockwise turn, and away it would come. The reflector stayed in position. Replace bulb, press rim, clockwise turn till click, and Bob was your uncle.

On my present car, first of all I have to undo four screws. And they're not ordinary screws, they're the ones with a cross in the head. They've got some special name, what is it again? Benson? Peters? Watson-Nicholls? Crunson? Bzazko? It'll come to me in a minute. The implied message from the LIA manufacturer is, 'we've put these Penfold (Crossley? Willis?) screws in with our special screwdrivers in our factory, don't *you* start messing about with them, you idiot consumer, you. But if you insist, you'd better start by going out and buying a Hotchkiss screwdriver of your own. And don't blame us if you can't get all the pieces back . . .'

Because when I am carefully easing out the last screw an incredible collection of springs and clips and fuss-gig fidgety-bits suddenly leaps out. Even when I've worked out how they go back it's impossible to do unless I could either get a little man inside the headlamps to hold two of them in place while I fix the third, or, alternatively, stand the car up on end.

The bulb itself is part of one of those complete LIA assemblies anyway, fixed from *behind* the reflector. This is a trick which the makers of ordinary hand torches have been quick to copy. They don't want you to be able to replace the bulb, or even the battery; they want you to buy a new torch. Preferably one encased in stormproof heavy-duty rubber, as though you were a coastguard forever being called out on wild nights. There is simply no way in to this casing, it isn't only stormproof, it's owner-proof.

But the LIA car manufacturers were only just beginning with my car headlights. With the new cars I see now, even if you had one of those screwdrivers (it *has* just come to me; *Phillips,* they are called)—even if you had a *Phillips* screwdriver it wouldn't be any use. I can't see any screws at all, the whole thing is flush with the body.

It's only a matter of time before the car comes completely sealed. You won't be able to open it even to *look* at the engine, let alone tinker with it or do something wild like change a fuse. Cars which let you do this are going the same way as cars with starting handles.

In fact, as far as cars are concerned, the rot began with

starting handles. My first car, which I was driving only 20 years ago, had this nice, short, blunt, business-like handle. It is true that unless you held it the right way—i.e. with your thumb on the same side as your fingers, a backfire could break your thumb. Or so it was said. But it was a snug feeling just *knowing* this, at any rate. Even if you couldn't start the car with the handle you weren't completely useless, at least you knew the right way to hold it.

But the LIA manufacturers began to make the handles longer, thinner, less and less functional, till suddenly—bingo! No car had any handle at all. If the battery's gone, Leave It Alone. Get a new one. Or at the least get an expensive tow.

The same goes for the brakes. On that first car if I wanted to tighten them I could tighten a knurled screw underneath the chassis (as we used to call it) which pulled the brake cable tighter. I knew where this screw was. Oily hands, a modest expertise, something achieved by *me,* on *my* car. They keep telling me they're 'self-adjusting' now; but every three months I have to leave it in the garage for a morning while they perform an intensely complicated operation called Bleeding the Master Cylinder. Bleeding the Owner, too, when he gets the bill. Or take record players. Gramophones, we used to call them; and it isn't only their name that has got longer and fussier. In the old days they were much simpler, now they're completely LIA. Then, when you wanted to change the needle all you did was undo a little screw, the old needle fell out and you put in another one from a little tin of 50.

Now the thing is called a stylus. Last month, noticing that my records were beginning to have a hoarse, scratchy background as though they were being broadcast from outer space and received by Jodrell Bank, I went to the shop where I bought the record player a year ago.

I thought it would be enough to tell them the make. Not on your life.

'What's the number on the cartridge?' they said.

Well, it's not the kind of thing you have in your diary,

along with Size of Hat, is it? I went home to have a look. Home is eight miles away, it was a month before I was in the shop again. They did a lot of poring in catalogues, explaining that there were now more than 400 kinds.

'You mean they come in 400 stylus?' I quipped. But they didn't laugh. Nor did I when I tried to fit it. I've never seen such a miserable fiddling little thing in such an imposing package. It reposed on a bed of foam rubber in a kind of plastic medal presentation case.

I'd rather they spent some of the money on instructions. Although if they did we'd have something like this:

1. Don't try to lift the tone arm to see what you're doing. It won't go any higher than that.
2. Just get the whole cartridge out of that stiff-looking clip arrangement at the end of the arm—*careful,* easy does it! Press with all the strength of your thumb but relax the moment you feel it give; otherwise you'll wrench one of these incredibly delicate-looking soldered wires. It's only fair to tell you it'll be even harder to put back.
3. Now get the old stylus out of the cartridge. What do you mean, you still can't see? Get a magnifying glass, or keep your record player in a north light.
4. Of course you'll have to force it out. It wouldn't play records if it wasn't held in securely, would it?
5. Well, use tweezers then. Eyebrow tweezers. Good heavens, surely you, or your wife, have eyebrows. Well, what do you tweeze them with? This contraption is just as delicate as an eyebrow. More so. It only weighs .00000001 of a gram, even if you did pay £1.30 for it. If it was any lighter it would float upwards.
6. The actual stylus bit that touches the record is almost invisible to the naked eye, and it fits into this itsy-bitsy little plastic thing. It's no fault of ours if this appears a different shape from the one you've just taken out. It's not rigid, it's supposed to wobble about like that, unless you've damaged it irreparably with those great fat fingers of yours. You're certainly no match for the

183

highly trained, nimble dwarfs we employ at our factory.
7. Go on, then, press it home—aah, look out! The WIRE! Now you've done it.
8. LEAVE IT ALONE.

The LIA philosophy is everywhere. Once I could mend a car puncture myself, now there isn't even an inner tube to *be* punctured. If the valve on my child's bicycle goes, it's no longer a matter of snipping off a little piece of valve rubber and fitting it, *oh* no. Leave It Alone, get a new valve. Any normally intelligent consumer, such as myself, used to be able to spot the odd loose joint in a radio or the odd valve in which the filament has stopped glowing—we even knew that some filaments didn't glow. But now who, except a boffin, can tell which transistor has gone wrong, or indeed knows which of those secret little square things *is* a transistor? How could the intelligent consumer find a loose joint in a printed circuit? What's he supposed to do, go out and consume another radio?

Just you watch it, manufacturers, or we shall really Leave It Alone in a way you won't like.

INVENT IT YOURSELF

In spite of the efforts of Dr Edward ('Lateral Thinking') De Bono, who goes round asking schoolchildren to design hypothethical things like 'a dog-exercising machine', it seems to me that inventors today have lost heart. I mean ordinary, adult, man-in-the-street inventors, who stumble on some divinely simple idea and instantly become rich, Part of inventors' folklore is The Man Who Made A Fortune From Putting Little Rubbers On the Ends Of Pencils. Nobody ever actually tells you what his name was. You are just left with this picture, as it might be of Harold Wimbush, or Henry Tomkins, or Adler Morton, or it may have been Charles Wibb, an insurance clerk, or was

184

it a tram driver—who got this idea, completely out of the blue.

And suddenly there he was, with a Victorian mansion set in rolling parkland, sherry on the terrace before dinner, a yacht, young men in some of the first open cars, smelling of sun-warmed leather, crunching up the gravel drive, walking under the great cedar tree towards the gay sounds of the tennis party on the other side of the formal garden and box hedges. George Cribb, or James Orniblow, or whoever he was, smiles at his wife Ethel as they recline in their wicker *chaises-longues*; they think that one of their three beautiful daughters is about to become engaged to one of the younger men, The Hon Cecil Ffolliot . . .

And all because of that little rubber. Not, mind you, that proper inventors invent primarily because they hope to get rich. They just have this marvellous, unquestioning optimism and faith in the idea itself. They might or might not get rich from it; what mattered was that they were the chosen instruments by which some now obviously Long-Felt Want was satisfied for the very first time.

Patent Office files are full of them in the golden, pre-plastic Age of Inventions, the 19th century. Anyone could have a go. A device with which anyone mistakenly buried alive could ring a bell from his coffin when he came round. Boots with the left sole of copper and the right one of zinc, so that with the acids in human sweat the wearer clumping along in them would form a living battery constantly recharged by his own electricity.

A rocking chair with a bellows underneath, connected, as the drawing with the patent application shows, to a vacuum cleaner used by a woman; while a man, smoking a pipe and wearing a smoking cap, rocks gently and reads the newspaper.

The preamble to an application by one Gustav Jaeger, of Stuttgart, begins, 'The scent or smell of the hair of healthy females possessing good digestion possesses energising and animal influence and is advantageous to the health'; (he had some way of *bottling* it).

Ideas ranged from the most grandiose ('volcanic heat

185

will be drawn into appropriate receptacles, furnished with tubes, to Industrial Establishments') to the most simple.

'The Preservation of Ferns. My invention,' says the application of Emily Walker Hunter, Bull and Mount Hotel, Briggate, Leeds, 'consists in simply ironing the fern in its natural state with a hot iron.' Of course, things still are invented in this century, but they tend to come from teams of professionals in white coats.

They periodically emerge from some huge subsidised laboratory and chant, like a Greek chorus, 'We have invented an organic condensation product which contains a multiplicity of structural units linked in series by amide or thioamide groupings, produced by a process of manufacture in which non-fibre-forming organic substances of lower molecular weight are converted into products of such high molecular weight as to be capable of being formed into filaments, which, on cold drawing, form a true fibre structure recognisable by X-ray examination.' This is the Patent Office definition of nylon.

Even Dr De Bono's child inventors seem affected by this. To a real amateur inventor (like myself) a dog-exercising machine would present no problems at all; you would simply need one of those static bicycles they have in gymnasia, only with a slightly adapted saddle and four pedals instead of two. But the children tend to produce huge machines, with many cogs and motors and chains, reminiscent of those which it was the official job of the late Nigel Balchin to examine when ideas for 'beating the bomber' were pouring into Whitehall during the emergency days of 1940. 'Very often,' he wrote in an unforgettable account, 'it turned out to be a Death Ray machine, usually a colossal apparatus which would cost about £2 million and divert a large part of the nation's war effort, although it was true that if you could get a German soldier to stand perfectly still in front of it, for 24 hours, *wearing a copper waistcoat,* it would make him feel pretty seedy.'

Whatever happened to those Long-Felt Wants? Do we really think there is no longer any need for simple inventions, such as A Method of Preserving Ferns, or having rubbers on the ends of pencils, and incidentally why can you now only buy full-length pencils too long for the pocket? What happened to those convenient little three-quarter-length ones with metal protectors at the point end, as well as a rubber at the other?

The BBC used to run a television programme called *Inventors' Club,* but to judge from the book of it, most of the ideas were curiously inward-looking, as though the inventors had somehow retreated from the great teeming outside world, with its tappable volcanoes, and people with electric boots, or even pencils, into a curiously claustrophobic, ever less adventurous and more fussily organised place called 'the home'.

In 'the home' they invented things like knives with holes in them (for scraping hard cold butter), a Face Mask for people learning the piano so that they can see the music but not the keyboard (cheating), a Music Silencer ('which can be attached to almost any musical instrument, reduces the sound to a point where it can only just be heard in the same room').

If they ever did venture out of this obsessively neat, labour-saving 'home' with its Self-Set Mouse Trap, its Reversible Scissors, its Saucer Ash Tray, its Combined Picture Hanger, Coat Hanger and Carrying Handle, they only went as far as the garden, full of feeble things like Safety Deck-Chairs ('the cross bar fits into the metal slots, and even if it should slip, it cannot reach further than the end of the metal rods').

You see? It's not the actual power of inventing that has been lost. It's just that the amateurs, the *true* inventors, intimidated by these laboratory teams of 'professional' inventors, have lost the confidence in their ability to answer Long-Felt Wants, and have dwindled into mere extensions of the do-it-yourself movement. Yet a little reflection will show that modern life provides us with an ever-increasing list of Long-Felt Wants (hereinafter referred to as LFWs). Everyone will have his own list, but here are some of the LFWs I intend to fill when I get a moment free from writing.

The Getter-up. There *have* been various half-hearted attempts to link alarm clocks with the bedclothes and little electric motors, but as everyone knows, the crucial moment in getting up is when one's torso is vertical; once one is sitting up, however blearily, one thinks one might as well get on with it.

My Getter-up would be a hinged bed of which the upper half would gently (but *gently*) move to a vertical position.

Orange Tester. Peeling an orange is a hell of a chore at any time, but if after all that trouble you find it is one of those all pale and withered at one end of each segment, tasting like rather old water, it is effort wasted into the bargain. My Orange Tester would be a thin needle that you could plunge into the orange, and a device at the end, like litmus paper, would show the pH, or whatever it is, that makes an orange *taste* like an orange.

Glasses Wiper. All the progress in miniaturisation and still no one has come up with tiny windscreen wipers for those who wear glasses! What are we supposed to do when it rains, stay indoors or keep bumping into lamp-posts? An LFW if ever I saw one.

Saliva-proof Plasters. For when you cut your tongue. I don't know about you, but I sometimes do this on the edge of envelopes when I'm licking them in a hurry. I've found that ordinary Band-Aids, though admirably waterproof as they claim, aren't saliva-proof, they just will not stick to the tongue, and also they don't taste like one's tongue. Mine would do that as well, so the wearer wouldn't be aware of them at all. They would of course be equally useful for people who *bite* their tongues.

Marmalade Knife. Two hinged flaps, operated by a small button on the handle, would come up, turning the knife into a rough spoon, while one was conveying the marmalade to the toast, and it wouldn't be able to fall off, the way it always does from an ordinary knife.

Once the knife was safely over the toast, moving the button the other way would cause the flaps to fold back flat on the other (that is to say non-marmalade) side of the knife.

Spirit-Level Bread Knife for Women. It has been known for centuries that women cannot cut a loaf vertically, leaving a flat surface for the next person. My knife would have a bubble-level on the handle; a de luxe version would flash a red light or ring a sweet-toned little bell when the knife went out of the vertical.

Flasher Periscope. All motorists know that of all the dad-fidgety, fiddle-twit, crackpate, pernickety, crotchety, dog-busted gadgets in the modern car, one of the most perverse and unpredictable is the direction flasher unit. Quite often the little green light can be twitching and ticking merrily away on the dashboard while no actual flash is being shown to the motorist behind, or perhaps the opposite to the one shown inside the car, or perhaps both, or sometimes a permanent green light comes on on both sides in the car, just when you are trying to change lanes on the M1. If you had my Flasher Periscope you would at least have visual evidence of what other motorists thought your intentions were.

New Smell Aerosol. I personally am never going to get into the new car league again, but one thing I recall from the time when for a brief heyday I did belong is that you get a brand-new *smell* in a brand-new car. It is compounded of fried paint (as it begins to burn off the brand-new exhaust and, quite possibly, green-painted engine block), new plastic, new carpet, and various faint rubbery sealant traces.

How comforting, once this smell had worn off after the first 1,500 miles, to be able to spray the car with it—in fact it would smell even more luxuriously new with my Aerosol, which would contain essences of rosewood, walnut and real leather, not just a smell of rotten old plastic.

Anti-Tit Device. To keep those birds out of the milk bottles. I had several ideas for this. A false top to the bottle, so that when the tit had pecked through there would be another top, just below its reach.

Or you could have an ordinary milk bottle with an

ordinary top but filled with cricket-boot polish (which tastes horrible, even to tits), and you could leave this out, instructing the milkman to leave the milk bottles in a different position relative to it each day, so that the tits wouldn't know which one to avoid, and this would give them nervous breakdowns. Anyone with a little scientific knowledge could invent things like this.

Perhaps we are getting nearer the laboratory-team type of invention with the *Sneeze Warning Device* (which would at least give you a chance to get your handkerchief out of your pocket).

Or the *Engaged Line Breakthrough,* enabling you to get through to someone who has been yacking away all day on his phone—or maybe someone has been yacking away to *him,* he would welcome the interruption. And what about one of the most obvious LFWs of all—the *Transistor Silencer*? Surely it's technically possible, sound waves being of a definite shape, to devise something that would instantaneously emit sound waves of exactly the opposite shape and thus muffle the blasted things—without of course anything having to be wired to the set (like that Music Silencer); public transistor players being the thugs they are, you can guess what a response you would get if you went up to one of them and said. 'Do you mind if I wire this up to your set?' No, *you* would have this beautiful device, unseen in your pocket, and you could watch the baffled rage on the moron's face as he shook his toy, trying to get the usual row out of it. I admit we're getting into boffin country now; but surely I have shown that there is still more than enough room for us all in the invention world. I'm too busy for it myself; but if anyone gets a mansion with rolling parkland, and so on, like that Roland Brigginshaw, or George Wragley, or whoever it was that put little rubbers on pencils, from any of these simple ideas, I hope he'll have the decency to invite me to a drink on the terrace, and I'll promise not to bother him about royalties. After all, there are plenty more LFWs where these came from.

I never saw anyone work so hard at relaxing as my friend Harblow. I never saw anyone spend so much on it, either.

He was the first man I knew to have an electric carving knife and an electric toothbrush. If they ever invent an electric comb or electric nail scissors, it will be for people like Harblow.

In his shed there are various spring-loaded forks and weird bent spades and other contraptions alleged to take the drudgery out of gardening. There's a kind of giant chromium-plated corkscrew on the end of a steel rod for weeding *while standing up*. If they ever get one for weeding while lying down, in a hammock, he'll have that too.

It's not that he's lazy. Far from it. He has to work hard to get the money to buy these things anyway; but he is a bachelor, with plenty of time to read all those articles about the strain of modern life, the importance of diet, the risk of sudden death to sedentary workers over 31, the need for daily exercise.

When he isn't working or exercising though, he demands *total* relaxation. He is always playing tennis, or swimming, or jogging, or doing graduated press-ups, while the rest of us are putting up shelves, or taking children to the zoo, or adding up the enormous grocery bill for the fifth time to find the mistake that must surely be there. For us, work fades imperceptibly into leisure—and that, according to Harblow, *is* the strain of modern life.

'I work hard and play hard,' he says, as though somehow the rest of us ate soft-centred chocolates all day while watching television in the office, and were always lying down taking naps on tennis courts.

'But leisure should be pure relaxation, a recharging of the batteries. So why not use science and technology to cut out unnecessary effort?'

This is why his house is full of remote-control devices—time switches, tea and coffee machines, dumb waiters, muted telephone bells; and of course a vast array of objects for sitting or lying on. It is scattered with huge harem-like cushions, although he is a bachelor; they're for *him* to recline on.

He was also naturally one of the first to buy, for pretty nearly £300, one of those black, buttoned leather reclining chairs with a matching footstool, associated with it the same way the dot is associated with the squiggle in a question mark.

Since he had spent all that on it, it took him much longer to admit to himself than it took me to find out, after one evening with it, that you cannot recline in one position. If you are in the *complete* reclining position, with your feet actually higher than your head, you get stiff behind your knees, you want to turn over and bend them, but the chair makes this impossible.

If you are reading idly, leafing through a newspaper or magazine, you want to lean back, but not too far back, otherwise your arms get tired holding up whatever you are reading. If this is a book with hard words in it you want to sit upright, dispensing with the footstool althogether.

For watching the television, yet another position is called for. Truly, man is a restless animal. As I pointed out to Harblow, tests have shown that the average person, during a night's sleep, changes position 183 times (or it may have been 283, I forget now. A lot, anyway).

Every time he wanted to change position (and Harblow is as restless as the next man; probably more so because he is always *asking* himself whether he's comfortable) he had to get out of this thing, or at least wrench at some lever and wriggle into the new position with an effort contrary to all his principles.

But this only spurred him on to something bigger and, of course, more expensive. The Functional Rest Unit (FRU) was the kind of furniture that only bachelors can afford to buy. It cost as much as a reasonable second-hand car and it was indeed a machine for relaxing. It was the only piece of furniture I had ever seen fitted with little electric motors and a control panel.

Harblow was hooked the moment he looked at the

full-colour brochure. 'The FRU is the ultimate triumph of ergonomic research, the study of human posture and movement,' it said. And there were several photographs of scientists peering at dome-headed Martian figures, made of wood and rubber, like the ones they use in car crash experiments, except that of course these were all just sitting comfortably.

Other photographs actually showed a skeleton reclining in the FRU.

'It must be just the thing after a hard day in the cemetery,' I said.

'You may laugh,' said Harblow. 'People laughed at Galileo, and the man who invented the umbrella. This is scientific. Look at those little wires coming from the joints.

'They're for measuring bone stress. These fellows have found out that if you sit or recline in the wrong position you do actual harm to your bones. That's what the green light on the panel is for; it shows when you are in the proper position for your body, with no bone stress. And everything is automatic, you simply press a button for any position you want. The stool is fully retractable . . .'

There was a faraway look in his eyes and I could see it was no use arguing with him. He ordered an FRU. And the next time I saw him was in hospital. He had broken his leg. 'Silly thing to do,' he said. 'I was sitting in the CR position . . .'

'The what?'

'CR. Concentrated Reading. More upright than RR—that's relaxed reading. A good big fat heavy book, it was. *The Rise of the Dutch Republic* by Motley.'

'I didn't know you were taking up history after all these years.'

'Oh well, it was rather a random choice, really, just to test the CR position. I hadn't tried it before. The position, I mean, not the book. Rather heavy going, actually. I was quite glad to put it down when the phone rang. I put it down and went to the table phone because I'd forgotten to switch it through to the chairside extension.

'While I was talking I noticed that the clock had

stopped, so I went over to the mantelpiece to rewind it, and I didn't notice that I had put *The Rise of the Dutch Republic* on the button that makes the footstool come out. It's retracted in the CR position, you see. So I tripped over it and broke my leg. So I know what I have to do when I get home.'

'Sell the thing to the Shah of Persia, I should think.'

'Good heavens, no. I shall need it more than ever now, to keep clear of bone stress, while the old leg is mending. No. I shall get an electric clock. Really an absurd waste of effort, all that winding.'

SCRUFFINESS IS IN

If it is not risking prosecution by that lunatic new government office in Manchester—the one that deals with sex equality—to say so, I believe that the modern unisex psychological pressure on men to pretend that they get pleasure out of buying clothes, just as women do, should be resisted.

For most men, buying clothes is a dismal matter of forking out good money—that could have helped towards the holiday, or a crate of wine, or even just the phone bill—for a whole damn new suit, when all that's wrong with the old one is that the right elbow has gone again and the cleaners say they can't Re-tex it any more.

Or it is a matter of being trapped in some discreetly lit, beige-carpeted, strip-lighted room on the first floor. One has gone in with the intention of buying the cheapest trousers they have, because one can actually see light through the right knee of one's present trousers while one is putting them on. If the waist is right the length is wrong, and vice versa. Of course, even if there is a pair which fits, they have not got it in the colour that goes with the jacket one is wearing, or any other jacket one has at home; and in any case, standing before the mirror, surreptitiously trying to bend the other mirror at an angle to it so that one can catch that elusive other-way-round profile which is, in fact, one's surprising real profile, that other people actually see, one is suddenly aware how scruffy and creased the jacket has become.

As if sensing this, a man with a tape measure round his neck springs out from behind a potted palm as one emerges, splendidly trousered, hung about with little tickets and cards with a lot of prose about washing in lukewarm water; and one is back in there again, trying on jackets of ridiculous splendour, lined with brilliant oriental fabrics. (And it's extraordinary how many times one seems to be taking one's *shoes* off and putting them on again, with these modern tight trousers.)

This is bad enough when one is alone. How much worse it must be for the sufferer when his wife or girlfriend is there with him too. I know exactly what that unhappy-looking man with the startling leading-the-winner-in-at-Newbury jacket over the shiny blue office trousers is thinking. He is thinking: what a Charlie I look, and can he *really* have said fifty-five pounds, my God; once I could have got eleven new suits with that.

It does not help him to have some woman, however dear to him, walking round him with pursed lips, pulling at the sleeves, murmuring—nay, saying out loud for all the shop to hear—'It's quite nice, but a little too full in the bottom for you, dear.'

What these women do not seem to understand is that two factors have now combined to make the buying of new clothes even more of an unhappy event for men.

The first is that it is even more galling to have to spend money on the perishing things just when we have arrived at a stage when scruffiness is socially acceptable . . . in younger groups indeed it is actually more socially accept-able than neatness. There are still some men who have (literally!) a vested interest in looking 'well dressed': salesmen for the better class of car, undertakers, insurance men, the representatives of large chemical firms, actors in the kind of play where people still *wear* clothes. But their numbers are dwindling.

The other is, of course, inflation. Now and again I find

195

myself passing a Gents' Outfitters and thinking absently, 'H'm, not a bad shirt for £4' (four *pounds*!) and then discovering that's just the price of the tie. How can men be expected to enjoy buying clothes at a time like this?

But there are deeper, more spiritual reasons. Men appreciate the fact that it is only when a garment has been worn many times that it achieves a certain human dignity, partaking a little in the soul of its owner, as well as his mere physical shape. The peasants in Van Gogh paintings, whom even now one can still see, doing something hopelessly unmodern, unmechanised, un-EEC, with sickles or rakes in Southern Europe still have this natural dignity because their many-times-washed clothes are practically a part of them; they are worlds away from the City gent walking stiffly along because he is afraid of bending the impersonal creases in his impersonal well-cut suit. Even the unisex-jeans crowd have recognised this fact by trying to sell new garments made to look old artificially.

I have only just stopped wearing, because the sleeves actually fell off, a coat which I am convinced helped me to write more with every year that passed (about 20 since I bought it). It got to look so like me that my wife took to saying to people who phoned when I was out (she wouldn't let me go out in it), 'I'm afraid he's out, but you can speak to his coat if you like.'

Men's liking for a garment follows an upward curve from the moment of its purchase (if it's any good at all and they haven't been shamed into buying something they know deep down is *wrong,* by the woman with them or by one of those fellows with the tape measures). It is just the opposite with women. The whole operation—the sight of the new persona in the mirror, the feel of the new material, the wrapping in the specially-designed carrier bag of the store, even the signing of the cheque—is a peak of pleasure from which there is a gradual declination, starting with the first time the thing is put on at home.

Eric Gill, the sculptor and typographer, once said that the best dressed women in the world were nuns (this was of course before Vatican II and all those smart calf-length,

196

couturier-designed habits). He said this 40 years ago, because he thought that male display was natural (look how dismal the peahen is compared to the peacock, or the female pheasant to the male). Of course in those days women outnumbered men, and now that the numbers are pretty well equal perhaps nature has decreed we have got to start being peacocks again, whether we like it or not.

If this is so, male clothes buying is going to get even more fraught than it is already, in two ways. No, in *three* ways.

First: advertising, and the whole slant of merchandising, will go through some kind of terrible sex-change. Male garments will be increasingly sold on their ability to present *men* as sex objects. As we go down the escalators, instead of all those girls in their underwear (already, you must admit, pretty hard-looking, either staring grimly out as if to say 'you needn't think *I'm* a sex-object, my good man', or actually smiling, *but with another girl*) we shall see posters for such things as Gorilla Shirts ('State bicep size when ordering; our exciting Gorilla range of wired bicep cups is planned to give *you* the muscle-fascination you have longed for, without pinching or riding round to the back of the arm').

'Mainly for Men, by Jim Brute . . . well, after the first flurry of the autumn shows, one tendency is clear; buttocks are out, the Stilt Line is in. George Smith is showing some wonderful straight-down trousers in pastel velours; the rear is a complementary colour to the front, and zips from top to bottom on each side, from hip to toe, mean that the trousers can be reversed to suit the wearer's mood. The meticulous stitching of the aggressive pockets is well up to the famous George Smith standards. They should be in the shops by the end of September.'

'The Swarthy Look is in! Once you have tried Bablon's new *Bluejowl Base Cream* you will know a new confidence; it stays 'fixed' through the most hectic evening. Good news, too, for men who suffer from sensitive ears; Harvery Watkins has designed a range of 'Jipsie' earrings which are cunningly attached by a remarkable new

197

adhesive, doing away either with painful piercing or the need for those worrisome little screws . . .'

Before this runs away with us any more:

Second: No doubt as a consequence of the foregoing, women (and, even worse, *girls*) will take to wearing monochrome semi-military suits of unvarying drabness.

Third: well, actually first, because it precedes the foregoing in time; it is something that is happening already. If women have not yet actually quite stopped dressing to please men, they are well on the way to making men dress to please women. You've only got to look at what has happened to dress shirts, which have already come a long way from a mere Georgette Heyer 'touch of lace at the throat and wrist', to veritable waterfalls, frilly and foaming, and in all the colours of the rainbow. You have only got to imagine someone like Robertson Hare in a caftan to see what a change has come about in our time.

Whatever you say about the old style of men's clothes, they were, on the whole, practical. Nobody is going to tell me those dinner shirts are practical; all they do is catch drops of gravy and wine. Even for ordinary daytime wear the women like us to buy those shirts with enormous standing-up collars, with huge fat velvet ties inside them, because they have this insane idea that we look comfortable and relaxed in them. *Relaxed*! They make the wearer hold his head up and keep his back more ramrod-straight than a guardsman (whose down-over-the-eyes peaked cap was at least designed to make him stand up straight, otherwise he would keep walking into lamp-posts; there was no rot about *that* being a comfortable garment).

James Laver pointed out that women's fashions through the ages have exploited different erotic areas of the body, and dress has always been a mate-attracting activity. If men are now going to have to do this instead of women, there is at least one consolation; once a man has got a mate, or the mate has got him, he can relax about it. In *War and Peace* Tolstoy draws us the contrast between the white-shouldered Natasha, charming all eyes at the ball, and the same woman translated into a comfortable, lumping young matron after her marriage. So look out, women; modern times may be with you in compelling us to waste our substance on these expensive fripperies, but once we are married we shall revert to type, in our comfortable old clothes, those old trousers and cardigans which, in the end, *become* us, in both senses of the word!

COCKTAILS WITH SOCRATES

There is no such thing as conversation at parties, if by conversation is meant the interchange of ideas, the marvellous mingling of minds by means of words, elegantly chosen, like pieces of mystical Meccano put together into some structure of lasting beauty or significance.

In the greatest conversation in the world, Plato's *Symposium,* it is easy for them to have this beautiful conversation because the guests are all reclining on their left elbows, not trying to stand up, holding a glass and a sausage on a stick. And there are only eight people, all allowed to speak in order.

Just let them try to organise that sort of thing at a party today.

PAUSANIAS: For my part, Socrates, I own that I find pornography boring.

SOCRATES: Have you then encountered a great deal of pornography?

BIG MAN IN BLAZER WITH MOUSTACHE: He loves pornography but he hasn't got a pornograph, ah HAH ha ha, hasn't got a pornograph.

PAUSANIAS *(ignoring this)*: No, Socrates, hardly any.

SOCRATES: Now in what may boredome be said to consist?

PAUSANIAS: I should say that boredom consisted in the lack of surprise.

SOCRATES: But is it not in the nature of a surprise to be instantaneous?

LADY WEARING ALMOND-SHAPED GLASSES *(with great earnestness)*: Oh, but I believe that a moment can be eternal.

SMALL BRIGHT LADY IN SMOCK: What was that marvellous thing, you know, in Oscar Wilde, when the man says this garden was intended to produce an impression of surprise in the visitor and the visitor says what impression is intended on a second visit?

HAIRY JOURNALIST: It wasn't Wilde, it was Peacock.

SMALL BRIGHT LADY IN SMOCK: Thomas Love Peacock, oh yes.

BIG MAN IN BLAZER WITH MOUSTACHE: Jane Love Tarzan, ah HAH ha ha.

SOCRATES: Let us get back to the question.

PAUSANIAS: I've forgotten what it was.

SOCRATES: Is it in the nature of a surprise to be instantaneous?

HAIRY JOURNALIST: What was that marvellous story in Peacock about the man whose wife found him in bed with the maid and said I *am* surprised and he said no, my dear, *we* are surprised; you are astonished.

SMALL BRIGHT WOMAN IN SMOCK: It wasn't Peacock, it was Lord Chesterfield.

GLAUCON *(suddenly)*: Yes, that is certainly true, Socrates.

SOCRATES: What is?

GLAUCON: Why, that surprise is instantaneous.

SOCRATES *(gratefully, recovering the thread)*: So, if boredom consists in lack of surprise, and surprise is instant,

HOSTESS: Ah, there you are, Glaucon. Now here's a young lady who's been dying to meet you; meet Miggy Twimble *(at least, that's what it sounds like)*.

HOSTESS *(to husband)*: Do try and get some of them into the other room. They *will* not start eating. Take Socrates with you, he's talking to himself again . . .

In real life, the party is sharply divided into those who have and those who have not something to say. All parties are attended by fundamentally three types of men and two types of women. The men are (a) non-talking, but tall,

200

confident-looking, with sensuous red lips; (b) eager and talkative, with thin lips, but secretly afraid they are talking too much, and wishing they had thick red lips; and (c) just naturally happy men called Billy or Monty to whom something funny has always just happened. The women are (a) beautiful, totally non-talking girls with sensuous red lips and (b) others. Maybe hostesses are right to keep everybody circulating after all. There would not be much conversation at all in that other room if all the (a) men were in there with all the (a) women.

PART FOUR

ENG. LIT. BITS

LITTLE ACORNS
*(on reading that a schoolboy essay by Graham Greene
had been sold at Sotheby's)*

....

WHAT I DID ON MY HOLDIAYS   by Greene, G.

I usually get dissapointed by holidays they expect you to be happy but think of all the dead things cast up by the Sea, the first day I found a dead starfish I took it to my room my Father said Poo it smells why don't you play with the other children in the hotel they are called Simpson. But there was another boy he had a dark face he watched us he said why don't we do something bad.

I asked him where are your Father and Mother he said my Father is with Miss Roberts she keeps gigling why does everyone gigle at the seaside his face wore an expression of disgust.

I always feel everybody is trying to escape from something at the seaside but they dont kno what it is and it makes them gigle they gigle in the hall of Mirrors and they put there faces in a round hole in a photograph of somebody elses Body and they gigle it makes me think of the dead Star Fish.

So I said all right to this boy his name was Lawrence he had an evil face. Let us go and look at the machines What the Butler Saw. He said Greene are you a Baby, I retorted with Spirit 'all right then, I know where the sewage comes out lets go and look at it poo it smells.'

He said nothing he looked at the Sea with Narrowed Eyes. Perhaps you would be happier with the Simpson children he said, it was an unspoken Bond. I know the back way in we can steal in and Drink the communion Wine he said. As we left the beach for the mean back streets we passed an old Man he was preaching his plackard said Repent ye Sinners thats my Father he's an old fool said Lawrence, I had a super holiday.

WHAT I DID ON MY HOLIDAYS   by Beckett, S.

I am going to write this essay on this paper with this pen about nothing because that is what the sea is it is nothing I like writing about nothing it is my favourite word here it comes agane woops nothing.

I think it look even better without a capitol letter, nothing looks more like nothing than Nothing with a captal letter. The sea is nothing strething to an illimmatable horizon. I kept staring at it in Killiney Bay that is where we went for our holidays we always go no change for Million years. I stood at the edge of the water I didn't paddel because I did not want to take my boots off because there were two tramps taking there boots off ugh poo they were waiting for somebody they said. The sea may be nothing but when I paddeled last year, the tramps were not there then, it was cold, so it must be something as well as nothing. I always knew that I bet I shall know it the same when I am Fifty or a Hundred or Two Hundred or a Million.

They were all lepping about on the strand, they shouted what are you doing I said nothing that's all there is here or anywhere else poo those tramp's boots!

When the tide came in I walked up the strand a long way, that was the way of it. Then I thought I saw a football in the nothing streching to that ilimmitable horizon. Then I saw it was not a football. I drew near and it was a man's head. I said Can you talk? He said of course I can talk. I have been here a million years. I said can you get out of the sand have you got a body but he started to cry and I went home we had Dublin Bay prawns for tea in the hotel.

WHAT I DID ON MY HOLDAYS   by Betjeman, J.

We had our holdiays this year
In Cornwall, spot to me so dear
The surf boomed in across the sand
And heather blossomed on the land

And in the hotel where we stayed
There was a garden where we played
Some girls were very strong and tall
And I could never win at all

We all had Aertex shirts and shorts
And gosh, I came to hate those sports
They hit me, then away they ran
With 'Yah, can't catch me, Betjeman'

We had our dinner every night
When it was only just still light
The sideboard groaned with HP Sauce
(Each family had its own of course)

And then with feet that seemed like lead
I went up oaken stairs to bed
But to sleep could never go
I heard them jabbering down below

They had red faces and plus-fours
They clumped upstairs and banged the doors
(It was a golf hotel you see)
And talked, I felt quite sure, of me

They saw their daughters beat me hollow
I knew what lines their talk would follow
They wondered what that boy would *do*
And just like them I wondered too.

. . . and an Imposition handed in by James, H.

I, since that is the nominative case and one is oneself the
actual (how could it be otherwise?) author (yet, again,
must not the application of this so made reverend term by
the mere accretion of centuries of respect—ah, yes, that at
least, respect, whether it be expressed as criticism or as
adulation—for the unique, the subjective process of mould-
ing a story, fine-spun out of, as it were, nothing, to one
who is already predestined to join that so revered, that so
Parnassian group, those very 'authors' but is in fact in all
the outward trappings of life a schoolboy, in itself
constitute a veritable, nay a fundamental misappropriation
of the word—the word 'author,' should the reader, no
matter how conscientious, have lost the thread, grammati-
cal for all its apparent yet so necessary circumlocution, of
this parenthesis, nor let that same reader, for whatever

scarcely-examined reason of grudge or incomprehension, suppose—ah, how mistakenly!—that this same, for want of a better, more conformable term, 'author', will by now have forgotten that this parenthesis is of an interrogatory nature of which it will—ah, so certainly!—be asked whether it ought not to end with a question mark, thus?) of these Lines (again, though refulgent poet-glories hang, as it were, about this word also, their connotation in the present instance cannot, nay must not, be untainted by all notions of a crime, of however inadvertent and unintentional omission) am obliged to confess that unless I can within the ever-narrowing space of words remaining to me, finish (ah, with what pain at its bluntness, its coarse insensitivity) with the congruent verbal phrase *must not forget my essay* I shall simply never manage the remaining 199 Lines.

POETRY TO SWEAR BY

There is always a feeling of anticlimax after a Poet Laureate has been appointed and the battle is over. Half regretfully one recalls the furious partnerships that gripped the nation; the march of 100,000 insurance workers behind their brass bands and banners to support Roy Fuller at a huge meeting in Bunhill Fields, the bloodied pates when a procession chairing Ted Hughes down the High at Oxford met one coming the other way led by Jill Tweedie and Brigid Brophy to advocate Mary Wilson; the frail figure of F. R. Leavis addressing a crowd from the steps of St Paul's in support of D. H. Lawrence; the Audenite meeting at Nuneaton when a crowd of ruffians supplied with gin by Spenderites cut the ropes of the enormous marquee in which it was held; the ten-day strike by Liverpool dockers in support of John Lennon, or was it Peter Lennon; the celebrated Larkin Cemetery Scandal; the emotional R. S. Thomas campaign that swept the Welsh valleys . . .

Now it is all over; each contestant, each supporter, in

true British sporting and poetic fashion, echoed in his heart the time-honoured phrase 'may the Betjeman win', and so it has proved. All parties look to our new poetic leader to heal the strife.

Yet he will have no easy task. In poetry, as in politics, we are basically a two-party nation; all Englishmen believe either that poetry should celebrate or curse. Yet it would be too simple an interpretation of Sir John's victory to see yet another triumph for the Celebrators, another defeat in the long succession of Cursers' defeats. He will not be unmindful of the words of Miss Jeni Couzyn, a member of the General Council of the Poetry Society, reported in *The Times* on the day that Cecil Day-Lewis's death was announced: 'Let the next Laureate be young, a poet still full of rage, who feels like a participant still, not an observer.' His majority was not so great that he can afford to ignore the vast though inchoate Cursers' party.

In other words, there will have to be some form of participation. The celebrationists have dominated English poetry for so long that it is easy to forget that but for a few historical accidents things might well have gone the other way, and many of our most famous lyrics would be somewhat different. Blake would have written:

Griping down the valleys wild
Griping wrongs of peasantry
In a crowd I saw a child
And he weeping said to me

'Gripe a song about a pain,'
So I griped one very drear;
'Griper, gripe that song again',
So I griped, he wept to hear.

Shelley forsook his Curser background to write joyful lyrics for which the Celebrationists gave him a luke-warm welcome that could never compensate him for the Cursers' hatred. Had he remained loyal some of his best-known lines would have been different. *To a Skylark,* for instance:

Shame on thee, blight Spirit!

Bird thou never wert
That from Hell, or near it
Pourest thy dull heart
In diffuse strains of unregurgitated art.

Liar still! Thou liar!
From the earth thou springest;
Stay down in the mire
That's where life is dingiest,
But singing thou dost bore, and ever
        boring singest . . .

And then of course there's Browning:

Oh, to be out of England now that April's here
(Or January, or Auguest, or any other bloody mouth)
And whoever wakes in England must each morning be
    aware
That the poorest house receives a bloody sheaf
Of tax demands, and tiny the relief
While the chagrin wrings his tortured brow
In England now . .

Of course none of these poets was Laureate, but there is
no reason to suppose that official, State-occasion poems
could not have been written in the Cursers' style by poets
full, as Miss Couzyn suggests, of rage:

On the Opening of Parliament By Our
Sovereign Lady The Queen

Well, it's a State Occasion. Oh my God
I suppose I've got to write about it
What a sod!
Well, I hope it rains on the First Carriage and Black Rod
And on the Second Carriage and the Ladies-in-Waiting.
I hope the leading horse's foot gets stuck in a granting.
Why the hell do the people cheer?
Military bands cost us seven million a year,
Here comes one now, everything from piccolo to tuba
God, it's boring. Now if it was the literacy campaign in
    Cuba

210

Or even just a little thing about what I did
In Madrid
I could write a poem
That would really show 'em . . .

There has always been some sort of loose connection
between Celebrationists and the Establishment, since
presumably the Establishment have more *to* celebrate.
Perhaps the ever-increasing demand for Curser poetry
could be met by some compromise, such as a poem
addressed to some resoundingly, professionally
non-Establishment figure:

Ode On the Birthday of Clive Jenkins

See where he comes, as Welsh as Cardiff Docks,
Compact of hwyl, and after-shave, and posh silk socks!
Lo, nymphs and shepherds dance, all sportive Nature
    laughs
With the Association of Scientific, Managerial and
Technical Staffs . . .

It is an interesting problem. Sir John is basically a
Celebrationist although he is by no means totally unsym-
pathetic to the Cursers. ('Come friendly bombs, and fall on
Slough'); it will be fascinating to see how he solves it in his
highly individual way.

THE COCKTAIL PARTY

The night I met T. S. Eliot, I was at a party full of tall
poets. My wife and I came, a little late as usual, to the
house of my publisher (that sounds a bit stilted. The pen of
my aunt, the hat of my father; the house of my publisher.
But looking back, as one can even at the start of a piece, I
think I put it that way because it sounds more, well,
objective, less as if I were claiming to be a poet—as might
appear if I wrote casually, right after that sentence about
tall poets, 'my publisher's house.' In saying 'the house of
my publisher' I am obeying a not altogether contemptible

211

instinct to establish this objective picture of the house, of the person taking our coats downstairs, of the sound of many voices coming from an L-shaped room on the first floor of this London house; the house, as honesty only now compels me to add, of my publisher).

Going up the stairs is partly like climbing Parnassus, wondering what all these poets will say to one when one gets to the top; and it is partly like that never-forgotten scene in *Citizen Kane,* with its sense of looking up at tall figures who cast shadows on a low ceiling.

Fortunately we find some friends among the lesser poets—smaller, chubbier poets not above, say, doing the commentary to a documentary film, a practice which gives us a tenuous common ground. But even while we are talking I am aware of these gaunt men all round me, a foot higher than I am, although I suppose they can't be really, since I am myself five feet eight inches.

Yeats, surely, was a tall man, although once a poet is dead one somehow stops thinking about his height. The only poet of whom I have an instant physical picture is Pope, simply because he was, of course, not tall, but crippled and small. And he, after all, wrote Augustan poetry in a London more graceful, more elegiac, more a *city* than it is now (what is it now?). Something wild again, a unity merely of streets, drainpipes:

Our street is up, red lights sullenly mark
The long trench of pipes, iron guts in the dark,
And not till the Goths again come swarming down the hill
Will cease the clangour of the electric drill

I don't see MacNeice here, but he probably is. If I find him I shall tell him that I know more actual lines of his than of any other poet in the room. Why does he get these slightly condescending reviews, often containing the words 'Mr MacNeice's poetic journalism'? Probably written by some tall reviewer, with a private income, who is in this very room (Louis worked at the BBC I wish I *had* told him now. He is dead, like Yeats. I don't remember him as being particularly tall).

Perhaps living poets, if they are any good, simply *seem* tall because they wrestle with the wild, with the receding infinite, they tie it up in heroic net-casts of metaphors, they force drastic human similarities on to chaos, they throw delicate wire bridges over the abyss across which we later tremulously follow them.

Of course, although all poets seem tall, not all tall men are poets. Nevertheless I feel pretty certain that nearly all these amazingly tall men here either do not have my anxious desire for the metaphors and compressions to be comprehensible, or else are a kind of men that finds *all* metaphors comprehensible, because of a superior mentality.

One should not be cautious, clearly. Poets should rave. The moment a thing is comprehensible it becomes a little dreary.

Yet these men are not raving at all. They nearly all have upper-class voices. Ha, there is one tall man who is not so much a poet as an editor. He is John Lehmann, and he is, I see, talking to Stephen Spender, who of course is a poet (and, come to think of it, an editor as well).

In this room there should be the beating of eagles' wings. So many tall poets. All the available poets in London are here, and there are some who have come in specially from Greek islands. In fact the whole evening has a very Greek flavour, because the party is in honour of George Seferiadis, who is not only the Greek Ambassador to London, he is also the poet George Seferis; and we are celebrating the publication of an English translation of his poems by another poet, Rex Warner.

My wife and I are introduced to Mr Seferiadis. I tell him he is the first ambassador of any kind we have met, let alone ambassador and poet. He smiles agreeably and we speak about the *dolmades,* the little Greek rolls of savoury rice in vine leaves. I am relieved to see that he isn't particularly tall. But then one doesn't think of modern Greeks as tall.

Surely there must be something that unites us all in this room, even the tall critics with their upper-class voices?

213

During a conversation with one of the chubby poets and his wife (we are trying to imagine some other ambassadors, past and present, writing poetry. What kind of verse would the late Lord Halifax have written? Sir Harold Caccia? Ribbentrop? Joseph Kennedy?) I think sadly, at the back of my mind, that I am never going to get into the class of these tall poets.

It is extraordinary to think that I once read *Antigone* and *Oedipus Tyrannus,* at school. But then, for various complicated reasons, I went into a factory that made telecommunications equipment, where I listened to oscillations in earphones all day long and filled in forms about decibel gain. Another three years and all that Greek would have stuck, whereas now the only line I can remember from either of them means 'thou art blind as to the eyes, to the mind and to the ears'. All the same, that's probably more Greek than some of the tall men in this room have— the poets, if not the critics, for if you are a critic you must know Greek. If you are a poet you must be a poet.

But it cannot be right, all this cultural classification. There must be something that unites us all. And just as I am thinking this there is an extraordinary wave, it runs right through the room. Without needing to be told we glance at the door. There is not actually silence, some social instinct ensures that a little low conversation goes on. But everyone knows, instantly, that T. S. Eliot has come.

I am certain no one in the room feels separated from Eliot because Eliot knows more Greek (or, come to that, Sanskrit), or because Eliot is a critic as well as a poet. All, all of us have looked through the exhaust fumes at the wild world, and, haunted by lost certainties, we have all felt:

Time and the bell have buried the day,
The black cloud carries the sun away.
Will the sunflower turn to us, will the clematis
Stray down, bend to us; tendril and spray
Clutch and cling?

He is, I observe, tall. But stooping now, for he has

214

recently been ill. It is shortly after his second marriage, he is leaning on his wife's arm.

How many here are like me, who if asked what single poem had affected them most, would instantly reply *The Waste Land*?—and then start qualifying, thinking of the *Four Quartets*? Night-school lectures, the objective correlative; enthusiastic walks home on windy nights, an overpowering sense of something real about to burst; the kingfisher.

From the wide window towards the granite shore
The white sails still fly seaward, seaward fly
Unbroken wings.

Voices unheard. He is in this room. And he spans the enormous Atlantic, he *is* the West; its trouble and ecstasy.

He sits with his wife on a settee in the smaller part of the L. People are introduced to him. Soon it will be our turn. What shall I say? *You have formed my soul?*

How absurd to be towering over him—he sitting, I standing. He cups his ear, I talk loudly. We are as if on a tiny white stage. Thousands, half seen in the blurred dark background, are listening. We are introduced. I hear myself speak.

'I bet I am the only man at this party who has to leave to catch the 8.30 from Liverpool Street.'

'Oh,' says Eliot instantly, 'where to?'

'Manningtree.'

'Oh, do you know why Falstaff is described as *roast Manningtree ox* in *Henry the Fourth*?'

'No, but I've often wondered myself. Of course it used to be a *wool* district, all those East Anglian churches are called wool churches' (shut up, as if he didn't know this already), 'but of course you never see a sheep there nowadays, or an ox. But there is a very good butcher in Manningtree.'

Then my publisher came up with someone else to introduce; some poet. And it was time to go and catch the train.

215

Until recently I was never quite reconciled to the thought that child prodigies do not run in our family. Look at all those Bachs—Johann Christoph, Ambrosius, Johann Sebastian, Karl, Phillipp, Phillipp Emanuel, Christoph Karl, Fridhelm, Wilhelm Karl, Michael Philipp, Johann Michael—not to mention Anna Maria Magdalena and their aunt (some scholars say their niece) Emily Bach, the trumpet player and inventor of marmalade. All tinkling, tooting, scraping or scribbling away long before they reached double figures.

Look at Mozart, playing the harpsichord at three.

Look at Lord Macaulay, who when he was eight wrote a *Compendium of Universal History* which gave 'a tolerably connected view of the leading events from the creation to 1800'.

Then look at my family. You'll have to look at them, because it would be no good listening, even though the money we've spent on music lessons over the years would have bought, say, a lakeside chalet at Lake Como, or three years' supply of champagne, or at least a Shiraz carpet with three conjoined stepped medallions in dark blue, 10 ft by 7 ft 4 in. And, charming though they are, some of them wouldn't know what a compendium *is*.

I used to be depressed by this until I saw a television programme about the Suzuki Method for teaching the violin, with crowds of Japanese children aged apparently about two-and-a-half playing the concertos of Vivaldi. Any child of reasonable intelligence could be taught to do this, it was claimed, provided the parents spent a lot of time on it too.

What do they think I've been doing all this time? I'd like one yen for every time I've said: "Look what *key* you're in, that's F *sharp*', or, 'Don't rush the bit you *can* play, that note is a crotchet.' Besides, I bet Japanese children don't burst into tears and bang the piano lid down when they get something wrong, or leave their violin on the

216

school bus about once a week, or lean on their flute as if it were a walking stick and bend it so that it only plays four notes and has to be repaired at a cost of roughly £27.

In any case, what's the point of being the *father* of an infant prodigy, especially if they are soon going to be a dime a dozen?

The idea of infant prodigies was once depressing because the whole thing was so rare and out of one's reach, and now it's depressing because soon it will be within *everyone's* reach. And that is why I have turned to a much more rewarding fantasy. I wasn't a prodigy and none of my children are; but I am going to be an Old Man Prodigy.

It will not be in any medium or on any instrument that I have previously tried. God knows, for instance, I tried on the piano; and for all the good it has done me I might as well be one of my own children. For a brief moment I could lurch through a few mathematical, dry, endlessly practised Bach pieces. But I knew, and my teachers knew, that I would never manage real pianism—lyrical torrents of Chopin or great banging sonorities of Brahms. I wasn't even a born player of *Pixies in the Glade,* or *Marching Along,* from *Six Easy Pieces* by someone with a name like T. Russell Cogforth.

So, I am going to be an old man prodigy on the cello.

I shan't start learning until I am 70, but by George the world will soon hear of me. At the very first lesson my teacher will look at me curiously. 'Are you sure you've never played the cello before, Mr Jennings?' she will ask.

She will be a beautiful young woman who has herself played the Haydn concerto at a Promenade Concert in London. But I shall be above that kind of thing, living only for my art as it rapidly becomes clear that this is what I was born for all those years ago.

She will soon (after about three months, I think) realise that there is nothing else she can teach me, and she will recommend me to *her* old teacher. I do not yet have a clear picture of him, except that he is some 30 years younger than I am and is the greatest player in the world. He lives in New Yor . . . no, stay, he lives in some lovely palm-fringed special school for master musicians on the coast of California. He has a great iron-grey mop of hair and speaks with an amusing Mittel-European accent.

On my second afternoon there, as soon as I have recovered from the jet-lag, I shall be running through one of the unaccompanied Bach suites in a cool practice room, heedless of the laughter and splashing coming from the nearby swimming pool. This will soon stop anyway, as, entranced by the flood of golden sound pouring from the open windows, handsome young men and serious-eyed beautiful girls, the cream of the world's young musicians, hastily dry themselves on the sunny patio and crowd in to listen.

They are so absorbed that they do not hear the slight gravel-crunch as an enormous white convertible stops at the bougainvilia-covered entrance. Out of it steps the oil and cattle millionaire Howard Jason Goldbrick, the chief benefactor of the school. Unnoticed, he joins the audience. I do not even notice there *is* an audience till I stop playing.

When the applause has died down Goldbrick says to my teacher, 'Witos, baby,' (yes, that's his name; Witoslaw Jercsy), 'I heard Casals, I heard Suggia, I heard 'em all, ain't it? But did yo-all ever hear a *portamento* like such a sound?' He has this rather mixed idiom because I'm not quite sure yet whether he is New York Jewish or a native of Baton Rouge.

'I came in with a question, like I was gonna ast you, *nicht war*? I seen where thisyer Guarneerius is comin' up for a private sale in Florence or some place; if you got anyone they's good enough to play it—but now you cayunt (yes, he *is* from Baton Rouge) tell me, I *know* it has to be this old guy. Where he-all come from?'

'H.J., I em tellink You', says Witoslaw, 'he vos all the time in Englant writink for the peppers mit liddle yokes and essays! Now he should laugh already, to find he is a genius from the bottom water! But ve must cry, he did not play such a beautiful for 50 years ago!'

H.J. will give me the Guarnerius on permanent loan. I

shall make my debut with it at the Lincoln Centre. My fame will precede me to London, where every seat will be sold for my recital in the Royal Albert Hall, which holds some 2000 more people than the Royal Festival Hall. Some of the finer points of my technique will be lost in its cavernous acoustics; but by now time will be getting short, and it will be necessary for as many people as possible to hear me in the few years that remain.

From a typical review of the period: 'No real music lover will want to miss the incredible "old man prodigy" Jennings. When Casals died none of us could have dreamed that the insights of old age, transmitted with perfect technique through the most poignantly eloquent of all instruments, would ever achieve a purer expression. But perhaps it is precisely because Jennings did not touch a cello, amazingly, till he was 70, that a knowledge of a wider world than that of a lifelong professional musician like Casals has given his playing this transcendently human quality. For the term of what most men would be glad to call their working life he was a minor journalist and writer, living on the perilous edge of obscurity, familiar enough with the Thoreau 'quiet desperation' of the lives led by countless millions of his fellow men. Perhaps only those who have such hard-earned knowledge of the plains and valleys can bring us the true exaltation of the summits. His account of the Bach Chaconne last night was more than a profound musical experience. It was. . . .'

But you *know* what it was. And I'll tell you another thing about this fantasy. If it hasn't actually worked out like that by the time I am 71, I can shift it forward ten years, to 81, and so on for as long as I'm around. I shall always have this dream to walk into. And that's more than those Suzuki children will have.